Excel 2

The Absolute Beginner's Guide to Maximizing Your
Excel Experience for Maximum Productivity and
Efficiency With all Formulas & Functions and
Practical Examples

By

HENRY SKINNER

REMEMBER that this book gives you access to 4 valuable bonuses.

At the end of the book you will find out how to get them.

Use them right now so you can make the most of the investment you have made.

Content

6

Introduction

The spreadsheet program Excel is a component of Microsoft's Office line of business applications. Microsoft Excel makes spreadsheet organization, formatting, and computation possible.

By structuring data using tools like Excel, data analysts and other users may make information easier to review as data is added or changed. Excel comprises a huge number of cells arranged in columns and rows.

The information will be placed here. Excel is a practical and frequently used tool integrated into and completely compatible with the rest of Microsoft's Office (including Office 365). The spreadsheet application runs on Windows, Android, Mac OS, and iOS devices.

The business environment is where Excel is most often used. It is used in various fields, including business analysis, operations management, HR management, and performance reporting. Excel heavily on pre-set cell formats to modify, store, and execute mathematical operations.

Graphing tools, pivot tables, and algorithms provide the ability to arrange data on a spreadsheet. The macro programming language used by the spreadsheet software is Visual Basic for Applications.

In MS Excel, several mathematical calculations may be made. Because it employs several formulae, it can simultaneously conduct operations on huge numbers, such as addition, multiplication, subtraction, and division. Additionally, it is easy to redo if the value must be increased or decreased.

Excel's formatting tools, such as highlighting, italics, colors, etc., allow businesses flexibility in showing and emphasizing important data. More than 10 million rows and more than 16 000 columns make up the Excel document. You may input more items, import data, and add photos through the insert tab. You may combine your data from many sources using Excel.

Excel is a crucial tool for managing a business. Excel use has gotten so widespread that even business owners use it. How Excel is used in business differs from one organization to another. A business may use Microsoft Excel for planning, budgeting, and other purposes.

Excel has enabled the business to effectively manage its daily operations. The Excel financial computations that the corporation used to make its decisions deserve a lot of credit for its success. Microsoft Excel's IF formula is particularly helpful for doing several computations in business usage logic.

Microsoft Excel is a fantastic resource for commercial purposes. Simply choose the templates menu to get all its features. You save time by not having to start from scratch when utilizing a pre-made template.

Everyone is in a hurry these days. They need to do several duties as part of their daily activities. However, to accomplish these activities, children must do some arithmetic. However, how can they easily do calculations? Excel has shown to be the most effective tool for managing this issue.

Excel speeds up complicated computations, which is advantageous for individuals and businesses. Microsoft Excel spreadsheet applications are highly popular. You will discuss your usage of Excel both at work and at home.

This chapter will go into great depth about Excel's capabilities, but first, you must comprehend how MS Excel works in general. This manual will assist you in mastering fundamental, sophisticated, often used, and employed functions and formulae.

Chapter 1: Microsoft Excel Basics

The most recent software release from Microsoft Corporation is called Excel 2021, and it comes with several new features that set it apart from early versions. If you are unfamiliar with Excel, let's briefly tour the program's key features.

1.1 What is Microsoft Excel?

Microsoft Excel is a spreadsheet program for storing and analyzing numerical and statistical data. You may execute tasks using Excel's equations, pivot tables, macro programming, graphing tools, and other features. Operating systems including Windows, iOS, Android, and Mac OS are compatible.

An Excel spreadsheet uses rows and columns to build a table. In most situations, alphabetical characters are assigned to columns and numbers to rows. The point where a column and a row meet are known as a cell. The address of a cell is composed of the letter denoting the column and the row number.

1.2 Why Should you Learn Microsoft Excel?

Every one of you uses numbers in your profession. Each of you has ongoing expenses you must cover from your monthly revenue. Understanding one's income and expenses is a prerequisite for making sensible investments. Microsoft Excel is a great tool for tracking, evaluating, and preserving numerical data.

1.3 Opening Microsoft Excel

Excel may be used in the same way as any other Windows program. Use Windows with a graphical user interface to do these tasks (Windows XP, Vista, 7, 8, 8.1, 10 or 11).

- From the drop-down option, choose **Start**.
- Illustrations should be a part of every program.
- Use Microsoft Excel as an example.
- Select **Microsoft Excel** from the drop-down menu at this point.

However, if it has been added to your **Start** menu, you may access it there. You may still access it using the desktop shortcut you created for it.

Microsoft Excel 2021 and Windows will both be used in this book. Press the **Start** button and then adhere to the procedures listed below to launch **Excel** on Windows:

- Press the **Windows** button on the monitor.
- By navigating the alphabetical list of programs, you may discover **Excel**.

- You may launch Excel without using the Windows **Start** menu by simply putting the word into the **Search** text field next to the **Window** button.
- When you press **Enter**, the app will display for you to launch.

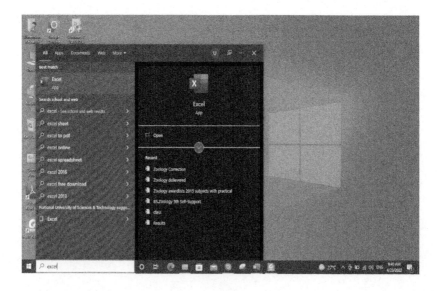

1.4 Closing Microsoft Excel

When you're done using Excel and want to shut it off, just follow these simple instructions:

- Press the upper-right corner's **Close** button while holding down **Alt** and **F4**.

1.5 Saving the document

You'll briefly go through the two ways you may use the Excel spreadsheet program to save the text.

Save: The save method is utilized whenever a new document is created. The file name and location must be entered in this box.

Save As: You may utilize the save feature as a tool to update a workbook that has previously been saved on your device. This command may duplicate a file, but to avoid overwriting the original, you must give the copied copy a new name and store it someplace else.

1.6 Microsoft Excel uses

The main benefit of Excel is that it can be used for various business operations, such as business intelligence, statistics, economics, data management, planning, reporting, product development, and invoicing.

Some of the services it will provide you include the following:

- Data storage & import
- Automation of the Tasks
- Number Crunching
- Charts & Graphs
- Templates/Dashboards
- Text manipulation
- & Much More

1.7 Terminologies of Excel

Workbook:

The workbook is a separate file, just like any other program. Each workbook has one or two worksheets. A workbook might have many worksheets or simply one worksheet. You may adjust the order in which worksheets appear in the workbook, add, or delete worksheets, conceal worksheets you don't want to remove, and more.

Worksheet:

The worksheet is divided into separate cells, each with the option to include text, a formula, or a number. This one has an inaccessible drawing layer and contains graphs, images, and diagrams. You may access all the worksheets in the workbook by clicking the tab at the bottom of the workbook window. Chart pages open by pushing a button and display a single heart may also be included in a workbook.

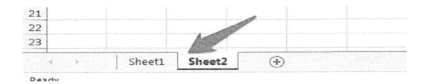

Cell

In a spreadsheet, a cell is where two columns and rows cross. Each cell in a spreadsheet is allowed to have any attribute that formula or virtual cell relation may access. You must insert the data into a cell if you want to utilize it in your worksheet. Now that a cell has activated, it may be altered.

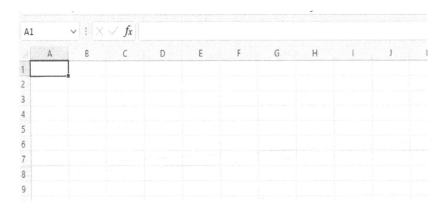

Rows and Columns

The columns and rows determine your cells' layout. While the rows are spread horizontally, the columns are orientated vertically.

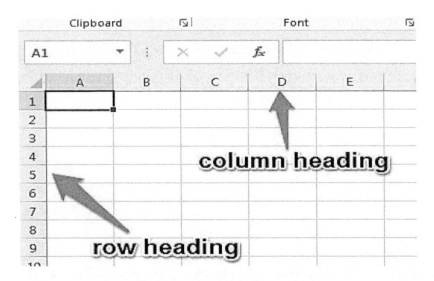

Rows Headings with Columns

Beyond the columns and rows are grey zones with numbers and letters that serve as the headers. The whole row or column is picked when you choose a heading. Additionally, the headers may change the rows' height or the columns' width.

Workspace

A workspace allows you to open many files simultaneously, much like worksheets in a workbook.

Ribbon

Above the worksheet is a row of control tabs called the **Ribbon**. Multiple possibilities are hidden beneath each **Ribbon** tab.

Reference Cells

A cell reference is a collection of standards that governs how a cell is classified. It is composed of both letters and numbers. For instance, **B3** designates the cell in row 3, column B.

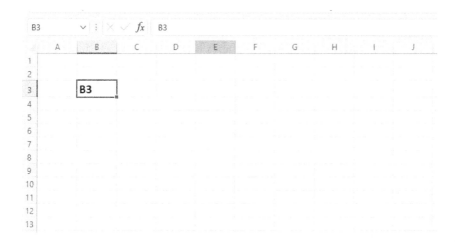

Range of Cells

A cell range is a collection of cells that have been arranged in different ways. Use a colon (:) between references to cells (:). The array, sometimes known as a range, was calculable by Excel.

The formula **A3:D3** instructs it to examine every cell in the box enclosed by columns A and D and rows 3 and 3, while **C4:F9** instructs it to examine every cell in the box enclosed by columns C and F and rows 4 and 9. A range that crosses many pages in the same workbook is a 3-D reference.

Merged Cell

When two or more cells are combined, a single cell is created.

Pivot Chart

The user may interact with the data by seeing graphical representations of the data in the pivot table using this chart as a visual reference for pivot tables.

Region of Pivot

You may relocate a pivot table field to alter how a report looks on the worksheet's pivot region.

Data Source

The data source is the source of the data used to create the pivot table. It might originate from the worksheet or a different database.

Values area

Value regions are the pivot table cells with the most recent data. These are subcategories of fields in the pivot table. Things might be the United States of America, Italy, or other nations if you have a Country field.

Template

A Microsoft Excel workbook or worksheet that serves as a template is made to help users finish a certain activity. Calendars, operating maps, and stock research all make use of templates.

Operator

The symbols and signs known as operators are used to designate which computations should be conducted in an expression. Examples of non-mathematical operators are comparison, concatenation, text, and reference.

Formula

A "formula" is a collection of letters used to create value in a cell. Beginning with the equal symbol (=) is required. Using a formula, function, cell connection, or operator is an option. A formula is often referred to as an expression.

Formula Bar

The **Formula Bar**, which is situated between the workbook and the Ribbon, displays the contents of an active cell. The formula bar in equations may display every component of the formula.

Function

Excel computations that have already been coded are known as functions. They are intended to simplify potentially difficult spreadsheet computations.

Formatting Cells

This changes a cell's or a component's visual representation in a spreadsheet. As you design the cells, their appearance changes; the value within the cells stays the same.

Error Code

Error Codes appear when Excel discovers a calculation error.

Filtering

Filters are guidelines that govern which worksheet rows should be shown. In these filters, information such as conditions or values may be employed.

AutoFill

The procedure of copying data to several cells is made simpler.

AutoSum

This tool totals the data on your sheet and displays the result in the cell of your choice.

AutoFormat

It's a piece of software that formats cells following predetermined standards. It may be anything as simple as a height disparity.

Validation of Data

This feature stops the spreadsheet from including unsuitable data. Data authentication ensures that the information provided is correct and dependable.

Table Pivot

It is a data summarization often used to dynamically arrange, aggregate, and sum data. One table contains the data, and another displays the results.

1.8 Microsoft Excel components

When utilizing the window for the first time, it's important to know where everything is. Therefore, you'll review each essential element before using Microsoft Excel.

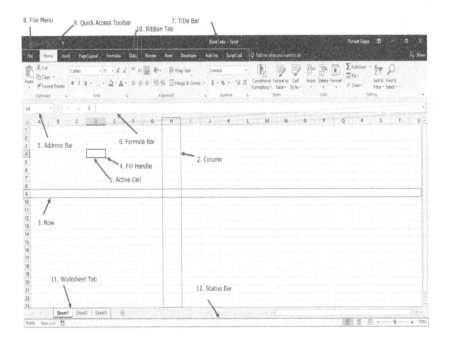

Active Cell

The selected cell is currently in use. It will appear in a rectangular box, and your address bar will display its address. You may alternatively click on it or use the arrow keys to activate it. To alter a cell, double-click it or press **F2**.

Columns

A column is a group of cells arranged vertically. Up to 16384 columns may be included in a single worksheet. A letter from A to XFD is used to denote each column. You may choose a column by clicking on its header.

Rows

While the columns are composed of cells arranged vertically, the rows are composed of cells arranged horizontally. There are a maximum of 1048576 rows in a single worksheet. A number between 1 and 1048576 uniquely identifies each row. You may choose a row by clicking the row number on your window's left side.

Fill Handle

The fill handle for the current cell is a tiny dot in the bottom right corner. It is useful for various tasks, including text sequences, ranges, numerical values, and serial numbers.

Address Bar

The address of the current cell is shown in the Address Bar. The address of the first cell in the range will be shown if you choose more than one cell.

Formula Bar

A formula bar often called an input bar, is underneath the ribbon. It enables you to view the content of an active cell and insert a formula into a cell.

Title Bar

The title bar would display the name of the application and each workbook's title ("Microsoft Excel").

File Menu

A file menu is a simple menu, much like many other programs. Additional options are available, including (Save, Excel Options, Open, New, Save As, Print, Share, etc.).

Toolbar for Quick Access

A toolbar that gives you quick access to the settings you want. Your choices may be added to the fast access toolbar when you add new options.

Ribbon Tab

Ribbons have taken the place of all option menus in Microsoft Excel since 2007. The option groups on the ribbon tabs each have extra options.

Worksheet Tab

This kind of tab shows all the worksheets in the workbook. The three worksheets in your new workbook have the default titles Sheet1, Sheet2, and Sheet3.

Status Bar

The Excel window's status bar is a little at the bottom. Excel will help you right away if you start using it.

Chapter 2: Designing Workbooks using Excel

There is at least one worksheet in each workbook. You can create several worksheets to better arrange your workbook and make finding things easier when working with a sizable amount of data. You may also group worksheets to apply data to several worksheets at once.

2.1 Rename Worksheet

One Sheet1 worksheet comes with a modern Excel workbook when you create it. The name of a worksheet may be altered to describe more accurately what's on it.

- Right-click each worksheet you want to rename, then choose the worksheet menu.

- Name the worksheet you wish to use in the appropriate field.

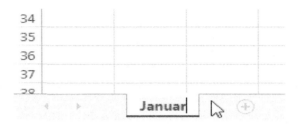

- Press **Enter** or use your computer and mouse to travel outside your worksheet. The name of the spreadsheet would be modified.

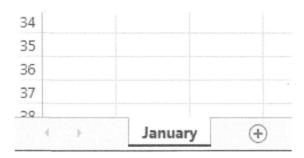

2.2 Insert A New Worksheet

- Click your "**New sheet**" key when you find it.

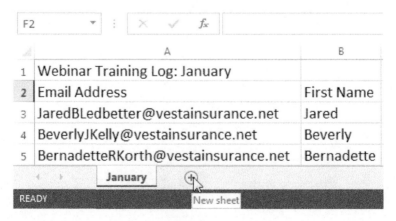

- The screen would display a fresh, empty worksheet.

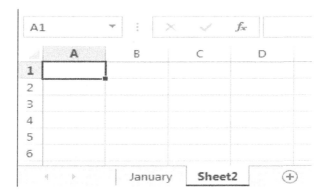

- Go to **Backstage preview**, tap **Options**, and choose the appropriate number of worksheets for each new workbook to change the default workbook count.

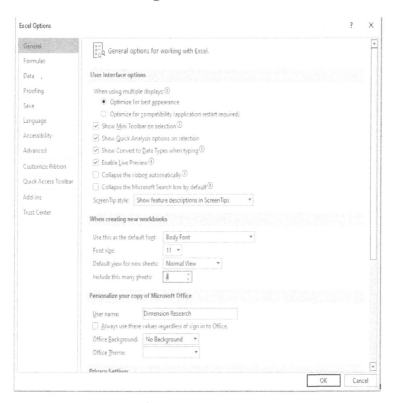

2.3 Delete Worksheet

- After right-clicking a worksheet, you want to remove, choose **Delete** from the worksheet menu.

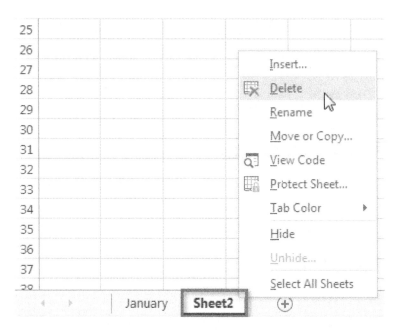

- The worksheet in your workbook would be deleted.

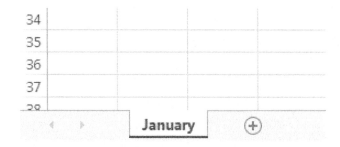

- By selecting the **Secure sheet** from the worksheet option when right-clicking the worksheet you want to protect, you may prevent certain worksheets from being changed or destroyed.

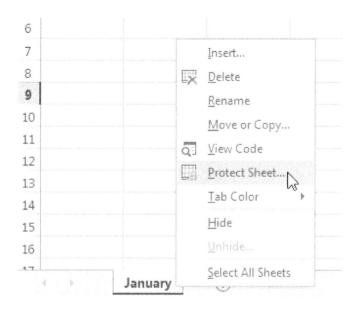

2.4 Copy Worksheet

It is possible to use Excel to replicate the contents of one worksheet to another.

Right-clicking any worksheet you want to copy will bring up the **Move or Transfer** option.

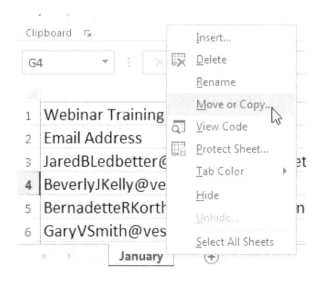

The "**Move / Copy**" dialogue box would then appear. Indicate where your sheet should appear in the Before sheet: area. You will shift the worksheet in this example to the right of the worksheet you are now using (move towards the end).

Choose to Create a copy from the drop-down option, then click **OK**.

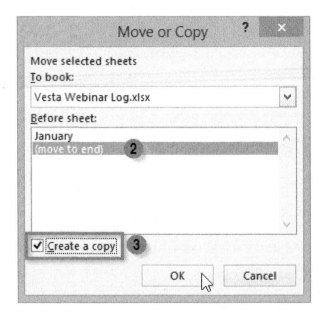

The worksheet will be duplicated. In your example, the January worksheet you copied would have the same name and version number as the original worksheet since you copied it (2). The information from the original January worksheet was repeated in the January (2) worksheet.

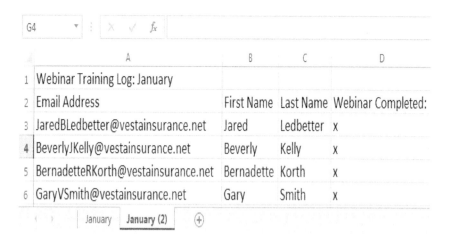

Another option is to copy a worksheet to another workbook. Any workbook that is offered is selectable from the book drop-down menu.

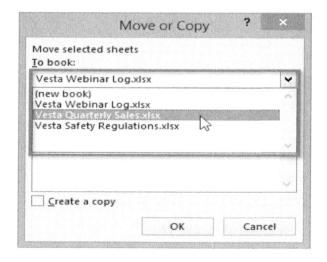

2.5 Move Worksheet

You may have to swap out worksheets if you want to rearrange the workbook. Select the worksheet that you wish to change. The cursor may change into a little worksheet symbol. Keep your cursor over the target region until you see a little black arrow.

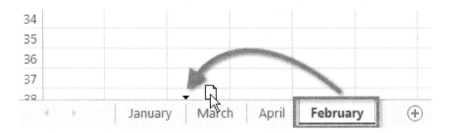

The mouse button should be released. A new location for the worksheet will be chosen.

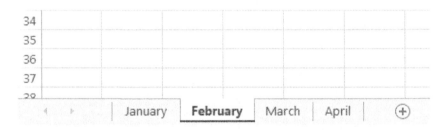

2.6 Change Worksheet Tab Color

Change the color of a worksheet page to better organize and make your workbook easier to use. After selecting the appropriate worksheet tab with the right click, move the mouse pointer over the Tab color. The screen would show a colorful menu.

Pick a color that appeals to you. The most recent worksheet tab color sample will show when your mouse hovers over different options. Red will serve as an illustration.

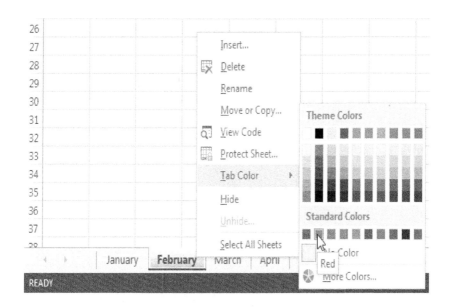

The tabs' color on the worksheet will change.

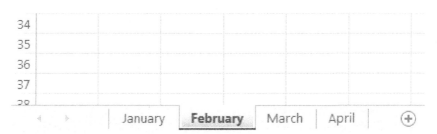

When you choose a worksheet, the color of the worksheet tab significantly diminishes. Choose a different worksheet to view how the color looks on a different worksheet.

2.7 Switching Between Worksheets

Using the tab, you may go to a different worksheet. To find the desired tab, you may have to go through all the tabs in larger workbooks, which can be tedious. Alternatively, right-click the screen's lower-left scroll arrows.

There will be a dialogue box with a list of all the sheets in the workbook. Double-click the sheet you wish to jump to after that.

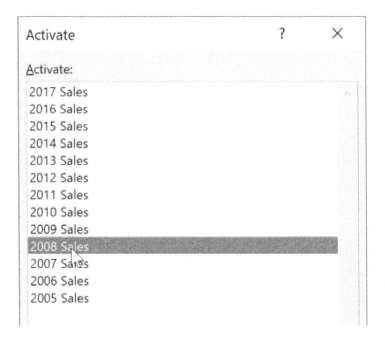

2.8 Grouping and Ungrouping Worksheets

You may do many worksheets at once or just one worksheet at a time. Worksheets could be combined to create a collection of worksheets. All worksheets in a category are affected by any changes you make to one worksheet in that category.

To group the worksheets:

In this situation, employees must get training every three months. You will thus create a worksheet category just for them. All the worksheets in a group are updated when you add an employee's name to one.

Pick the first worksheet to add to the category of worksheets.

Your keyboard's Ctrl key should be depressed.

From the drop-down menu, choose the group's subsequent worksheet. Pick worksheets one at a time until you've chosen every worksheet you want to arrange.

Ctrl should be released. Your worksheets have been grouped at this point.

After sorting it, a worksheet inside a category may be explored. The other worksheets in the group would automatically update any changes made to one worksheet. If you need a worksheet that isn't a part of the community, you'll need to ungroup every worksheet.

To ungroup all worksheets

By selecting Un-group from the context menu when right-clicking a worksheet, you may access sheets from the worksheet menu.

Groups of worksheets would be created. To ungroup the worksheets that aren't already in the group, click on one of them.

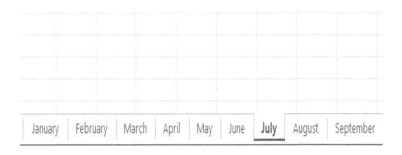

It is possible to group and ungroup worksheets. Group your January and March worksheets if you're following along with the scenario. Compare a January worksheet to a March worksheet after adding new information.

2.9 Page Layout View

You may want to open the worksheet in the **Page Layout** view to examine your page layout modifications.

- Clicking on the instruction to examine **Page Layout** will take you to the right bottom corner of your worksheet.

Page Orientation

Excel has two-page orientations: landscape and portrait. The portrait is vertically orientated, while the landscape is horizontally oriented. When dealing with several rows, a portrait is the finest option; the landscape is the ideal choice when working with numerous columns. Portrait orientation performs best when there are more rows than columns in a spreadsheet.

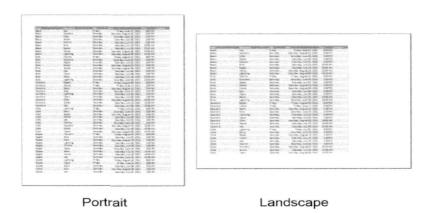

Portrait   Landscape

To change page orientation:

- Choose the **Page Layout** tab from the **Ribbon**.
- The drop-down box labeled **"Orientation"** offers the options "**Landscape**" and "**Portrait**."

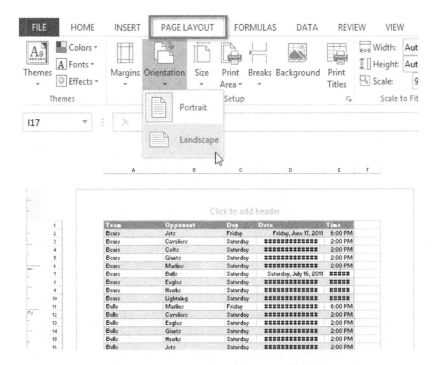

The page orientation of the workbook will be changed.

To format page margins

It is the space between the text and the edge of the page. All workbooks start with this default configuration, which leaves a one-inch space between the content and page boundaries. You may need to fiddle with the margins a little if your data doesn't exactly fit on the page. Excel has a variety of predefined margin sizes.

- Choose the **Margins** to command option from the **Page Layout** menu on the **Ribbon**.
- Select the proper margin size from the drop-down selection. You may choose **Narrow** if you want to add more content to the page.

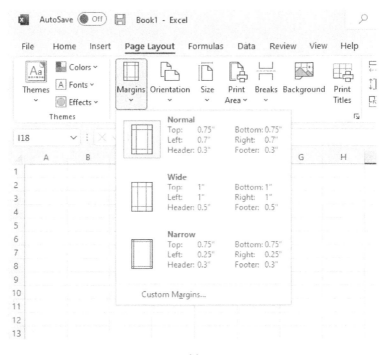

- The margins would then be adjusted in this situation to accommodate your new option.

To use custom margins

Additionally, you may modify the margin size in Excel's Page Setup dialogue box.

- Under the **Page Layout** menu, choose **Margins**. **Custom Margins** is an option that you may choose from the drop-down menu.
- Will the Page Setup dialogue box appear?
- After that, press **OK** to see your changes.

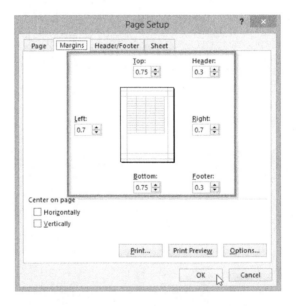

- The margins of the notepad will be changed.

To include Print Titles

Ensure that each page of your worksheet has a copy of each title heading to print a full copy. It would be hard to interpret if the title headings were only included on the first page of a printed workbook. Print Titles instructions let you choose which rows and columns to display on each page.

- From the Page Layout option on the Ribbon, choose Print Titles.

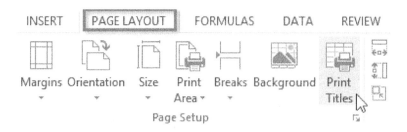

You will now see Page Setup so you can edit your page. From here, rows and columns might be duplicated on every page. In our situation, a row will be repeated.

Selecting a **Collapse Dialogs** button next will reveal the rows that will repeat at the top.

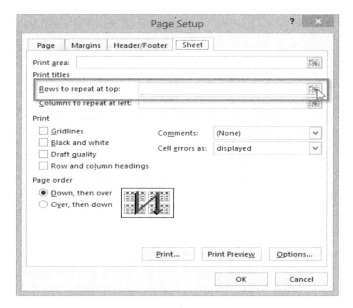

- The **Page Setup** dialogue box is collapsed, and the mouse cursor is replaced with a little selection arrow. Choose the rows you want to repeat to have the same row on every printed page. Take row 1 for the sake of an example.

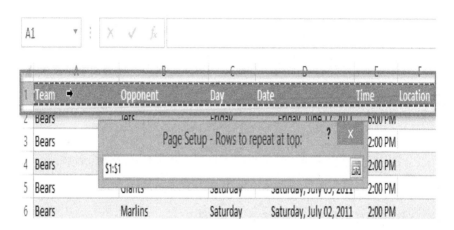

- Row 1 will be added into the Rows for repeating at the top: field. It's time to turn on the "**Collapse Dialog**" again.

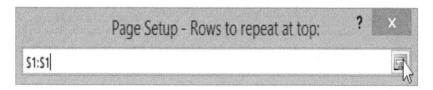

- Expand the **Page Setup** dialogue box. To confirm your activity, press the **OK** button. Row 1 will be placed on top of every page.

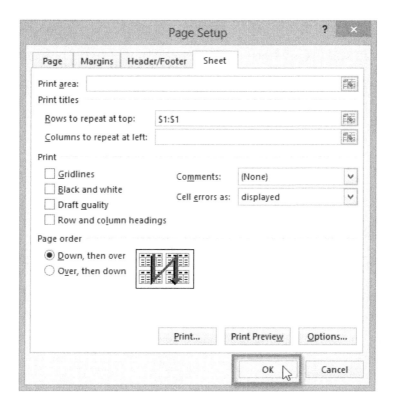

To insert a page break

You may print different parts of your worksheet on different pages by adding a page break to your workbook. Both horizontal and vertical page breaks are possible. Horizontal and vertical pages break into separate columns and rows. In this example, a horizontal page split will be used.

- You may find and select this command to display **Page Break Preview** here. The worksheet will be shown in **Page Break** mode.

- Choose the appropriate check box, then click on the row in the area where you want the page break to occur. You may add a page break by choosing row after row 28. (In this case, 29).

	A	B	C	D	E
19	Bulls	Lightning	Saturday	Saturday, June 18, 2011	10:00 AM
20	Cavaliers	Eagles	Friday	Friday, August 05, 2011	6:00 PM
21	Cavaliers	Hawks	Friday	Friday, June 17, 2011	6:00 PM
22	Cavaliers	Bears	Saturday	Saturday, August 13, 2011	2:00 PM
23	Cavaliers	Bulls	Saturday	Saturday, June 25, 2011	2:00 PM
24	Cavaliers	Lightning	Saturday	Saturday, July 16, 2011	2:00 PM
25	Cavaliers	Tigers	Saturday	Saturday, July 02, 2011	2:00 PM
26	Cavaliers	Colts	Saturday	Saturday, August 20, 2011	10:00 AM
27	Cavaliers	Giants	Saturday	Saturday, July 23, 2011	10:00 AM
28	Cavaliers	Jets	Saturday	Saturday, July 09, 2011	10:00 AM
29	Colts	Lightning	Friday	Friday, July 01, 2011	6:00 PM
30	Colts	Bears	Saturday	Saturday, June 25, 2011	2:00 PM
31	Colts	Eagles	Saturday	Saturday, August 13, 2011	2:00 PM
32	Colts	Hawks	Saturday	Saturday, July 30, 2011	2:00 PM
33	Colts	Jets	Saturday	Saturday, July 23, 2011	2:00 PM
34	Colts	Marlins	Saturday	Saturday, June 18, 2011	2:00 PM
35	Colts	Cavaliers	Saturday	Saturday, August 20, 2011	10:00 AM

- You may insert a page break by choosing the **Breaks** option under the **Page Layout** tab on the **Ribbon**.

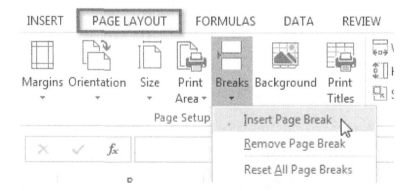

- There would be a page break indicated by a dark blue bar.

	A	B	C	D	E	F
19	Bulls	Lightning	Saturday	Saturday, June 18, 2011	10:00 AM	
20	Cavaliers	Eagles	Friday	Friday, August 05, 2011	6:00 PM	
21	Cavaliers	Hawks	Friday	Friday, June 17, 2011	6:00 PM	
22	Cavaliers	Bears	Saturday	Saturday, August 13, 2011	2:00 PM	
23	Cavaliers	Bulls	Saturday	Saturday, June 25, 2011	2:00 PM	
24	Cavaliers	Lightning	Saturday	Saturday, July 16, 2011	2:00 PM	
25	Cavaliers	Tigers	Saturday	Saturday, July 02, 2011	2:00 PM	
26	Cavaliers	Colts	Saturday	Saturday, August 20, 2011	10:00 AM	
27	Cavaliers	Giants	Saturday	Saturday, July 23, 2011	10:00 AM	
28	Cavaliers	Jets	Saturday	Saturday, July 09, 2011	10:00 AM	
29	Colts	Lightning	Friday	Friday, July 01, 2011	6:00 PM	
30	Colts	Bears	Saturday	Saturday, June 25, 2011	2:00 PM	
31	Colts	Eagles	Saturday	Saturday, August 13, 2011	2:00 PM	
32	Colts	Hawks	Saturday	Saturday, July 30, 2011	2:00 PM	
33	Colts	Jets	Saturday	Saturday, July 23, 2011	2:00 PM	
34	Colts	Marlins	Saturday	Saturday, June 18, 2011	2:00 PM	
35	Colts	Cavaliers	Saturday	Saturday, August 20, 2011	10:00 AM	

- When viewing your worksheet in **Normal** mode, a solid grey line denotes an additional page break, whereas a dashed grey line denotes an automatic page break.

To insert headers and footers

Headers and footers make your worksheet easier to understand and give it a more professional look. The worksheet's header and footer are located at the top and bottom, respectively. Headers and footers often include identifiers such as page numbers, dates, and workbook names.

- The command to see **Page Layout** is located at the very bottom of the **Excel** window. The worksheet will appear when you are in Page Layout mode.

- Select the header or footer you want to change. There will be changes to this page's footer.

- A new tab named **Header & Footer Tools** will appear on your **Ribbon**. You may find commands with dates, page numbers, and workbook names here. We'll add page numbers to this example.

- The footer will automatically provide the page numbers.

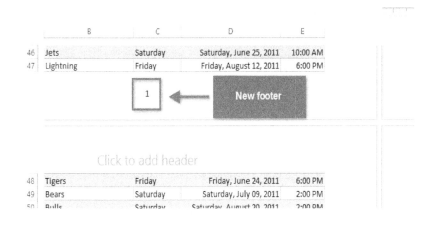

Chapter 3: Data Management in Excel

You'll begin working on the worksheet in this chapter. The skills from this chapter are often employed when making a workbook out of one or more worksheets.

3.1 Editing Data

Your Formula Bar allows you to double-click a cell to edit its data. You could have seen that when you input the data, it was written into the cell at the location designated by the Formula Bar. You may add new data into cells and edit previously entered data using a formula bar. How to enter data into a cell location and then change it is shown in the steps below:

- Click **cell A15** on the worksheet for **Sheet 1**.
- After inputting the abbreviation Total, press the **ENTER** key.
- Simply select **A15**.
- Move the mouse cursor up to the Formula Bar. The cursor will take the place of the pointer. Move the cursor to the end of the acronym Tot and then click it.
- To complete the word **Total**, add a few more letters.
- Select the checkbox next to your **Formula Bar** on the left. The modification would then be recorded in a cell.

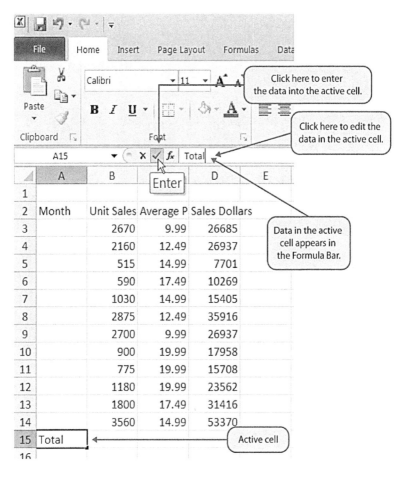

- Double-clicking on **Cell A15** is required.
- Add the word Sales, separating it with a space after the word **Total**.

Start by pressing the **ENTER** key on your keyboard.

Shortcut Key for editing Data into a Cell

You may modify a cell by selecting it and pressing the F2 key on your keyboard.

3.2 Remove Data

Use one of the following techniques to eliminate a cell from a worksheet:

- From the list, choose the cell you wish to delete.
- Choose the appropriate option, then choose the **Delete** command from **Ribbon's** home tab.

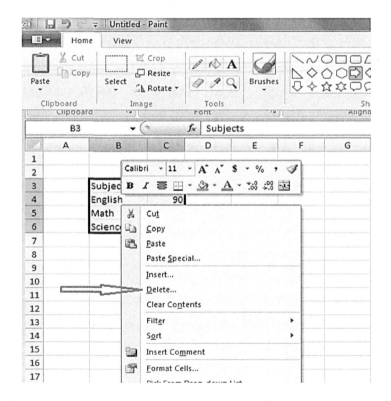

- After everything is done, the cell will instantly move higher.

3.3 Cell Content Copy Pasting

It is necessary to follow this process.

- Pick the information from a cell that you wish to copy.

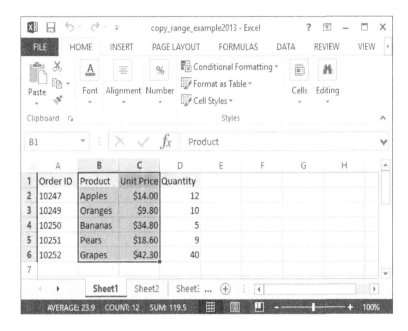

- From the home page, use the Copy command (or **CTRL+C** if you want).

On the **Home Tab**, locate the area where you want to paste the data, then click **Paste**. Remember that the copied cell may have a dotted box around it for labeling (you may paste by using the keys **Ctrl+V**).

3.4 Cell Drop and Drag

To avoid the stress of cutting, copying, and pasting, you move items from one cell to another by dragging and dropping them. To do so, adhere to the following guidelines:

- Pick the cells that you wish to move.
- Drag the mouse along the border of the cells you've selected to pass the contents of those cells.
- By using the mouse to click, hold, and drag the cells.
- The cells will move to their right location after you release the mouse.

3.5 Use of Fill Handle

When moving data from one cell to the next in a spreadsheet, Excel's fill handle may help you save time. Using the fill handle, you may quickly copy and paste a cell's contents onto other cells in the same row or column.

Use the fill handle as directed by these steps:

- The fill handle may be seen as a little square in the bottom right corner of the selected cell when choosing whose material to imitate.

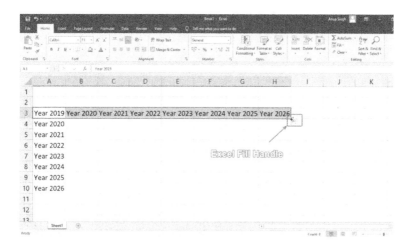

- To fill all the cells, you want to fill, select, hold, & move the fill handle.
- After that, let go of the mouse button to fill the chosen cell.

The fill handle may also be used to start a day series or a sequence of numbers (1,2,3). (Monday, Tuesday, Wednesday). Most of the time, you'll have to select many cells before using this fill handle.

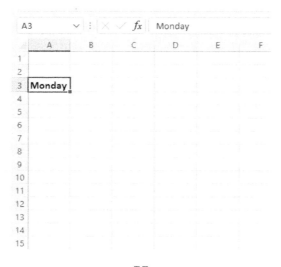

See the pictures below to learn how to begin a sequence using the fill handle.

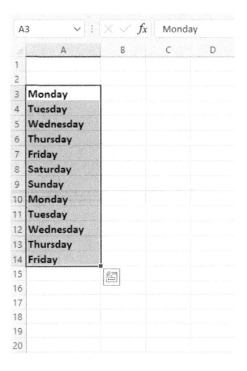

3.6 Adjusting Columns and Rows

Your worksheet's entries are missing from some of them. For instance, the last letter of the word September is hidden in the A11 cell. This is because the phrase cannot fit in the column. The Excel worksheet's columns and rows may be adjusted to fit the data in the cell. The steps below describe how to configure column widths and row heights in a spreadsheet:

- Move the mouse pointer between Column A and Column B in spreadsheet Sheet 1. A white block + may be used to create two arrows.

- Click and drag the column to display the whole word September in the A11 box. When you adjust the column, a recommendation box for column width appears. The number of characters that would fit in the column using the standard font and size, Calibri 11-point, is shown in this box.
- Release the left mouse button to complete the action.

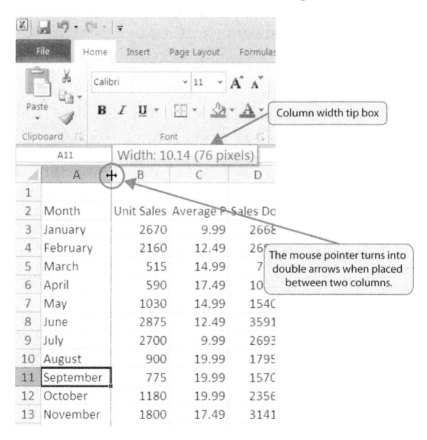

You'll notice that the click-and-drag method is ineffective if you wish to alter the width of a certain character for one or more columns. A second method for changing column widths by utilizing a certain number of characters is shown in steps 1-6:

You may choose any cell location in A Column by dragging the mouse pointer over the cell and then hitting the left mouse button. You might also highlight the positions of cells in several columns if you use a comparable character width for each column.

- Select a **Format** button by left-clicking it in the **Cells** group on the main **Ribbon** tab.
- Make your selection for **Column Width** from the drop-down menu. A dialogue box will show the column width.
- Enter **13** and click **OK** in the **Column Width** dialogue box. This value will determine the character width in the A Column.
- To enable **AutoFit**, move your mouse cursor back to Columns A and B intersection until you see a double arrow. Depending on the maximum entry for the column, the column's width is altered.
- Utilizing the **Width** of the **Column** dialogue box, increase the column's width to 13. (See the thread's step 6 here.)

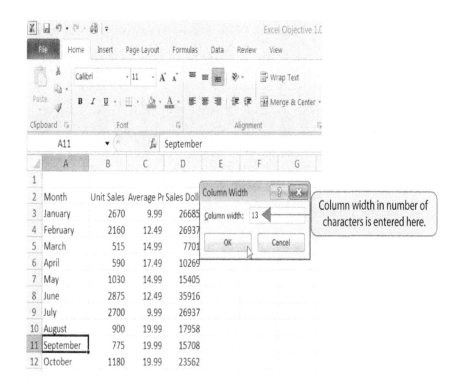

Column Width

Once you're at the keyboard, press **ALT**, then the letters **O**, **H**, and **W**.

Change the row's height in steps 1 through 4, equivalent to changing the column's width.

- To pick cell A15, position the mouse cursor over it and then click with the left mouse button.

- On the main tab of the **Ribbon**, left-click the **Format** button in the **Cells** group.

- A **Row Height** option may be selected from the drop-down menu. The **Row Height** dialogue box then appears.

- After entering **24** into the **Row Height** dialogue box, click the **OK** button. The height of row 15 will now be 24 points. The diameter of each point is 1/72 of an inch. Increasing the row height provides more room between the worksheet totals and the remaining results.

Row Height

- Once you're on the keyboard, press **ALT**, then the letters **O**, **H**, and **W**.

The worksheet in the image below has Row 15 and Column A modified.

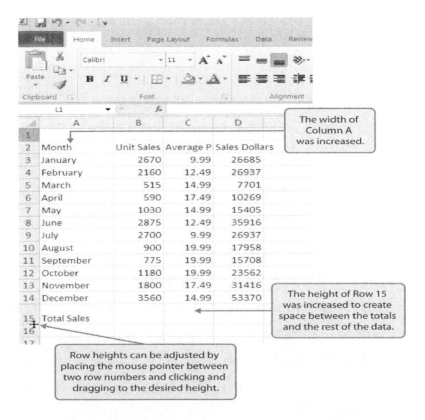

The width of Column A was increased.

The height of Row 15 was increased to create space between the totals and the rest of the data.

Row heights can be adjusted by placing the mouse pointer between two row numbers and clicking and dragging to the desired height.

3.7 Cell Formatting

There are several cell formatting possibilities, so we'll go through how to apply them here with some simple guidelines.

Modification of Font

Calibri is the default typeface that shows when you launch Excel for the first time. This font emerges when you enter letters, numbers, and other characters into cells in an Excel spreadsheet. You may change the typeface on the main tab to whatever font you choose to make it easier.

Follow these steps to do this:

- Select the cell where you want to make the font change.

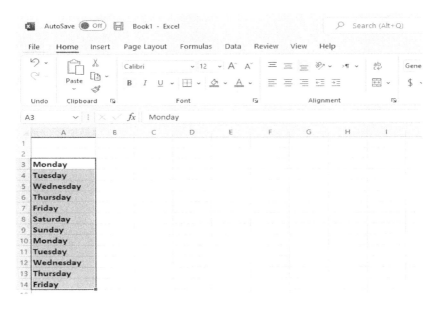

- Select the **Font** command from your home page, then select the proper font.

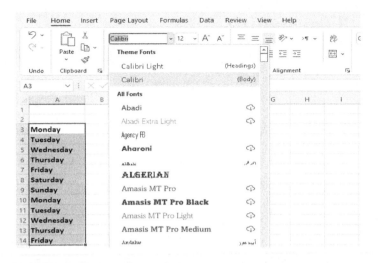

Change font Size

Use these instructions to change the font size:

- You only need to choose the cell whose font size you wish to change.

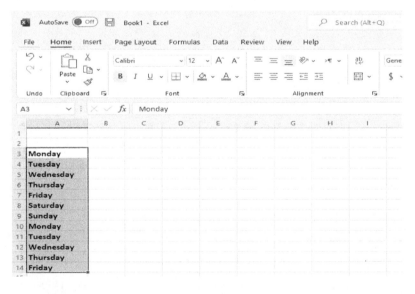

- Change the font size to your preference by selecting the **Font** command from the home menu.

Changing Font Color

Simply do the following to modify the text color in your cell:

- Select the cell whose text color you wish to change.

- By choosing the **Font Color** option under the **Home** menu, you may change the font size to suit your preferences.

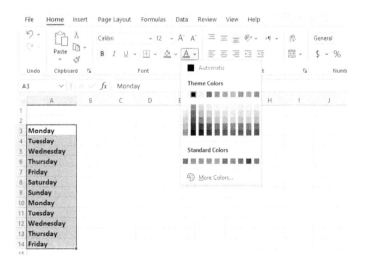

- When you're done, the font's color will have changed.

Commands in Bold, Italic, and Underlined

- Choose the cell where you wish to alter the font color. Choose **bold**, **italicized**, or **underlined** instructions under the home tab to make the necessary changes.

Background color addition with fill color

The cells will have a background color thanks to the fill color, making them stand out from the worksheet. The background of the cell may be whatever color you choose.

- Select the cell to which you wish to apply the fill color to achieve this.

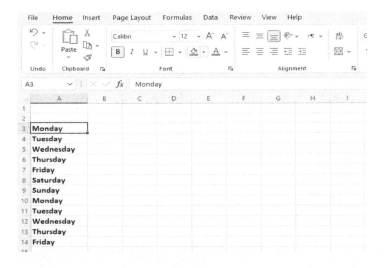

- Choose the appropriate color from the **Fill** color drop-down option on the Home page.

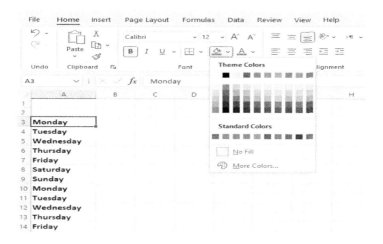

Adding Cell Border

A worksheet's border allows you to separate the cells from the rest of the page. To add a border, do the following:

- Select the cell that needs editing.

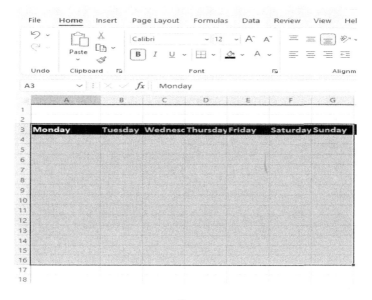

- You may pick the required border style by navigating the Home tab and choosing the **Borders** command.

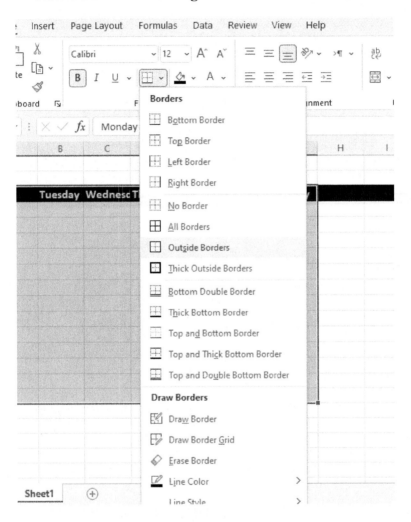

- The border you choose will be seen in this tab.

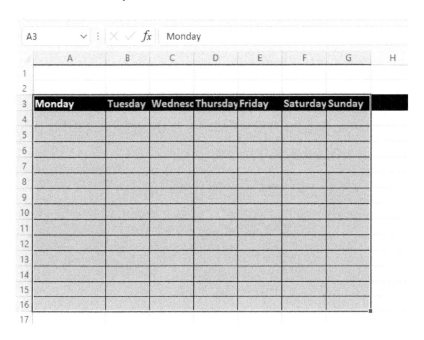

Changing Border Text Alignment

By design, the text typed into the spreadsheet has always been centered in each cell. You'll alter the appearance of your cell content to make it simpler to read. Simply take the following actions to change the alignment:

- Select the cell that needs editing.
- Go to the **Home** tab and choose the **Align** function to pick the one you want.

3.8 Conditional Formatting

With conditional formatting in Excel, you may modify a cell's color depending on its value.

Highlight Cells Rules

To call attention to cells whose values surpass a certain threshold, utilize the following steps.

- You have the options of **A1** through **A10**.

	A	B
1	14	
2	6	
3	39	
4	43	
5	2	
6	95	
7	5	
8	11	
9	86	
10	57	
11		

- In the Styles category of the Home tab, choose Conditional Formatting.

- From the drop-down selection for the **Highlight Cells Rule**, choose **Greater Than**.

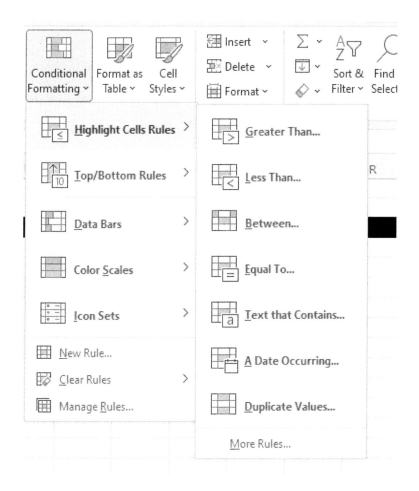

- Select a formatting option, then type **80**.

- Choose the **OK** option.

Result

- Excel indicates in bold any cells with a value greater than **80**.

	A	B
1	14	
2	6	
3	39	
4	43	
5	2	
6	95	
7	5	
8	11	
9	86	
10	57	
11		

- Set the value of cell **A1** to **81**.

Excel, therefore, automatically modifies the format for cell A1.

	A	B
1	81	
2	6	
3	39	
4	43	
5	2	
6	95	
7	5	
8	11	
9	86	
10	57	
11		

Notably, this category may also draw attention to values that are less than, between, or equal to the value, cells that include a certain string of text, dates (such as right now, previous week, next month, etc.), duplicates, or unique values.

Clear Rules

To remove the conditional formatting rule, follow these steps.

- The **A1:A10** range may be selected from the drop-down menu.

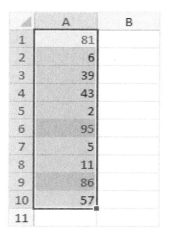

- On your **Home** tab, choose **Conditional Formatting** under the **Styles** heading.

- To remove rules from selected cells, choose **Clear Rules**.

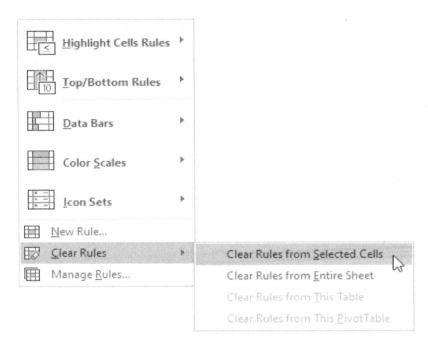

Top/Bottom Rules

Use the following procedures to identify cells that are above average.

- Choose the range **A1–A10**.

	A	B
1	81	
2	6	
3	39	
4	43	
5	2	
6	95	
7	5	
8	11	
9	86	
10	57	
11		

- Choose the **Conditional Formatting** option on your **Home** tab under the **Styles** section.

- From the **Top/Bottom Rules** drop-down box, choose **Above Average**.

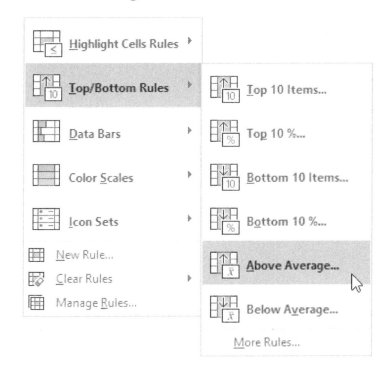

- Select a formatting style for your content.

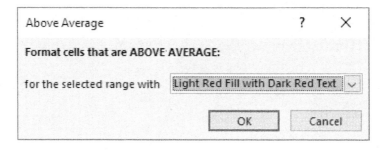

- Choose the **OK** option.

Result. Excel prepares any cells that are greater than the average (42.5).

	A	B
1	81	
2	6	
3	39	
4	43	
5	2	
6	95	
7	5	
8	11	
9	86	
10	57	
11		

Notably, you may use this category to draw attention to all top-n items, top-n percentages, bottom-n items, bottom-n percentages, or cells below the average.

Conditional Formatting with Formulas

To improve your talents with Excel, use a formula to specify which cells you format. Formulas for conditional formatting must evaluate as TRUE or FALSE.

- Choose a range between **A1** and **E5**.

	A	B	C	D	E	F
1	90	77	33	20	96	
2	59	66	20	61	44	
3	94	99	97	41	52	
4	36	43	70	13	54	
5	15	6	28	28	15	
6						

- Choose the **Conditional Formatting** option on your **Home** tab under the **Styles** section.

- Select the **New Rule** button.

- Choose "**Use a formula to select which cells to format from the drop-down box.**"
- Type your formula here: = **ISODD (A1)**
- After choosing a formatting style, click **OK**.

Result

- In Excel, Excel highlights any odd figures.

	A	B	C	D	E	F
1	90	77	33	20	96	
2	59	66	20	61	44	
3	94	99	97	41	52	
4	36	43	70	13	54	
5	15	6	28	28	15	
6						

Explained: Always enter your formula in the upper-left cell of the designated range. The formula is instantly transferred to several more Excel columns. Consequently, the formulas for cell **A2** and cell **A3** are respectively = **ISODD(A2)** and = **ISODD(A3).**

Here is another example.

Choose the **A2–D7** range.

	A	B	C	D	E
1	Last Name	Sales	Country	Quarter	
2	Smith	$16,753.00	UK	Qtr 3	
3	Johnson	$14,808.00	USA	Qtr 4	
4	Williams	$10,644.00	UK	Qtr 2	
5	Jones	$1,390.00	USA	Qtr 3	
6	Brown	$4,865.00	USA	Qtr 4	
7	Williams	$12,438.00	UK	Qtr 1	
8					

- Retrace steps 2-4 once again.
- Enter **"USA"** in the formula box by typing =$C2.
- After choosing your formatting type, click **OK.**

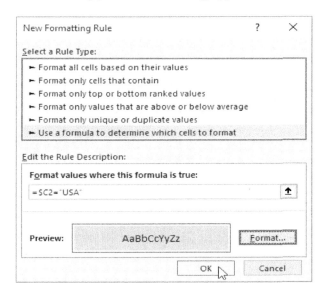

Result

- In Excel, every order from the United States is underlined.

	A	B	C	D	E
1	Last Name	Sales	Country	Quarter	
2	Smith	$16,753.00	UK	Qtr 3	
3	Johnson	$14,808.00	USA	Qtr 4	
4	Williams	$10,644.00	UK	Qtr 2	
5	Jones	$1,390.00	USA	Qtr 3	
6	Brown	$4,865.00	USA	Qtr 4	
7	Williams	$12,438.00	UK	Qtr 1	
8					

Adding a dollar sign ($) in front of the column letter ($C2) will allow you to correct your reference to column C. As a result, cells B2, C2, and D2 have the formula **=$C2="USA,"** whereas cells **A3, B3, C3,** and **D3** have the formula **=$C3="USA".**

3.9 Cell Merging and Text Wrapping

When working on the worksheet, you can see that a cell has too much content, leading you to wrap the cell or blend it instead of enlarging it. Because the text in the cell is scale wrapped to fit the cell, the cell may be altered, and the information can be shown on several lines. You may join or merge similar cells to produce a bigger one by merging.

Utilize the following when combining cells:

- The cell you wish to merge should be selected.

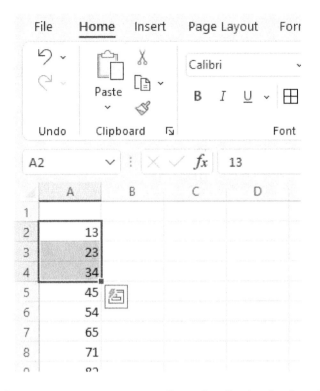

- Select **Merge & Center**, then the desired selection from the list, all from the **Home** menu.

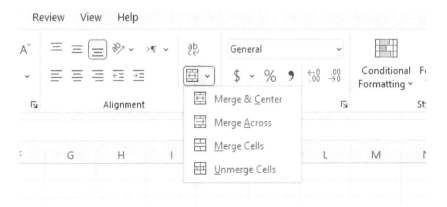

- After that, the cell will be modified to reflect the selection.

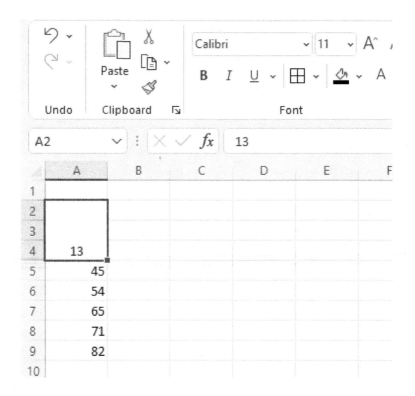

For wrap texts

- Choose the cell that you want to wrap.

- If you choose text using the **Home** tab's **Select Text** command, the text in the cells will be wrapped.

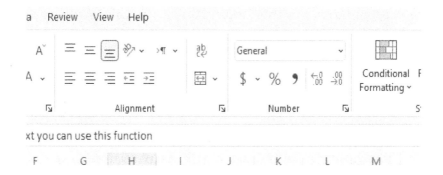

xt you can use this function

- The contents of the compartments will be wrapped.

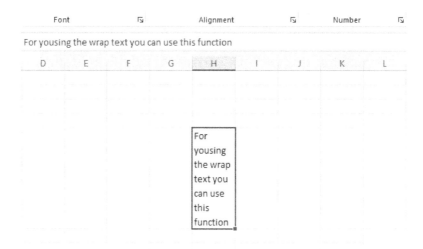

3.10 Hiding Columns and Rows

In addition to modifying the worksheet's rows and columns, you should also hide them. It's a great method for hiding information you don't need to see while enhancing your spreadsheet's visual appearance.

To illustrate these points, a spreadsheet containing information on GMW sales would be utilized. However, there are no secret rows or columns on this spreadsheet. In this case, certain powers can only be shown.

- Putting the mouse pointer over **Sheet1's C1 cell** and pressing the left mouse button.
- Click the **Format** button on **Ribbon's Home** tab.
- Put your mouse pointer on the **Hide & Unhide** option in the drop-down menu. There will be an options drop-down menu shown.
- The settings submenu has a hide Columns option. The result of this is that **Column C** will be hidden.

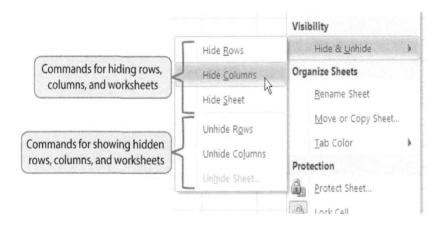

Shortcut key for hiding columns

- While pressing the **0** key on the keyboard, keep holding down the **CTRL** key.

The C Column in the spreadsheet is hidden in the Sheet1 worksheet. The absence of the letter **C** causes the column to be hidden.

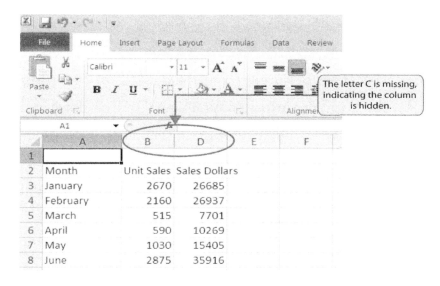

To display the column, follow the procedures below:

- You may highlight the **B1:D1** range by activating cell B1 and moving it to cell D1.
- Click the **Format** button on **Ribbon's Home** tab.
- Hover your cursor over the **Hide & Unhide** option in your drop-down menu.
- **Unhide Columns** may be selected from the options submenu. The C Column would then appear in your spreadsheet.

Shortcut Key for unhiding column

- To highlight the cells on each side of a hidden column, click the closest parenthesis key on the keyboard while holding down **CTRL** and **SHIFT**.

The following techniques demonstrate how to conceal rows in the same manner that you may conceal columns:

- Clicking the left mouse button while the mouse is over the A3 cell on your Sheet1 worksheet.
- Select the **Format** key from the main tab of the **Ribbon**.
- The **Hide & Unhide** options in your drop-down menu should be highlighted with your mouse. A drop-down menu of options will appear.
- You may find **Hide Rows** in the supplied options' submenu. Row 3 would become invisible as a result.

Shortcut key for hiding rows

- Click the number **9** on the keyboard while holding down the **CTRL** key.

To find the dispute, follow these steps:

- The **A2:A4** range is emphasized by activating the A2 cell and moving it to the A4 cell.
- Press the **Format** key on **Ribbon's Home** tab.
- Move your mouse pointer over the choices for concealing and unhiding the drop-down menu.
- **Unhide Rows** may be chosen from the **Options** submenu. You may now see the third row on your worksheet.

Shortcut key for unhiding rows

To highlight the cells above and below the hidden row, hold CTRL and SHIFT while clicking the **(()** key on the keyboard **(s)**.

Hidden Rows and Columns

Most workers are used to using one another's Excel spreadsheets. When utilizing a worksheet generated by someone else, look for any hidden columns and rows. You can quickly determine whether a column or row is buried if a column letter or row number is missing.

Unhiding Columns & Rows

- The cells above and below the secret row(s) and the cells on the left and right sides of a concealed column are highlighted (s).
- The **Home** tab of the **Ribbon** must be selected.
- Select the **Format** key from the Cells group.
- Put the pointer over the options for hiding and unhiding.

From the drop-down menu, choose **Unhide Rows** or **Unhide Columns**.

3.11 Adding new rows and column

Add new row

- From the drop-down menu, choose a row heading, then place it where you want your newer row to appear.
- To see the new lines, go to your **Home** tab, choose the insert command, then tap on the Insert sheet row.

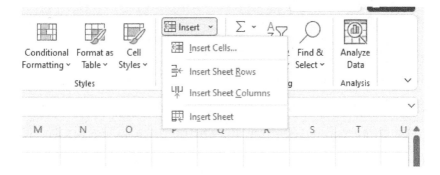

Add a new Column

- Choose the right-hand column heading wherever you want the new column to appear.
- Choose the **Insert** command from the **Home** tab to see the new sheet, then tap on the **Insert Sheet Columns**.

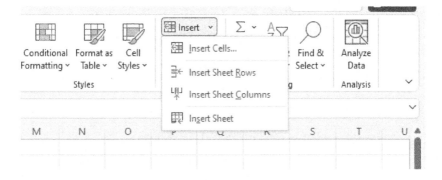

3.12 Removing Columns and Rows

Simply follow these steps to eliminate a row or column that isn't being used:

- Select the unwanted rows and columns and click **Remove**.
- On the main screen, click the **Delete** option to remove the required rows and columns.

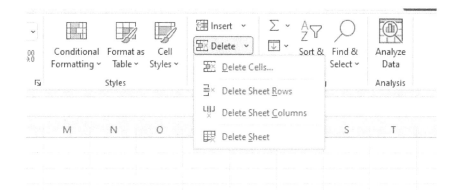

3.13 Transpose (rotate) data from rows to columns or vice versa

Simply follow these steps to eliminate a row or column that isn't being used:

- Select the unwanted rows and columns and click **Remove**.
- On the main screen, click the **Delete** option to remove the required rows and columns.

Sales by Region	Europe	Asia	North America
Qtr 1	21,704,714	8,774,099	12,094,215
Qtr 2	17,987,034	12,214,447	10,873,099
Qtr 3	19,485,029	14,356,879	15,689,543
Qtr 4	22,567,894	15,763,492	17,456,723

Tables may be switched around to show sales regions on the left and quarters in the column headings, as seen here:

Sales by Region	Qtr 1	Qtr 2	Qtr 3	Qtr 4
Europe	21,704,714	17,987,034	19,485,029	22,567,894
Asia	8,774,099	12,214,447	14,356,879	15,763,492
North America	12,094,215	10,873,099	15,689,543	17,456,723

Please be aware that the Transpose function won't be available if data is kept in the Excel table. Either use the **TRANSPOSE** function to rotate every row and column or convert your table to a range first.

Here's how you can do this:

To select the data you want to rearrange and any column or row labels, press **Ctrl+C**.

By choosing a new place for the transposed table in the worksheet, you can ensure enough space for your data to be pasted. The new table you enter will replace any information or formatting in the current one.

To paste a transposed table, just right-click on the cell and choose **Transpose** from the context menu.

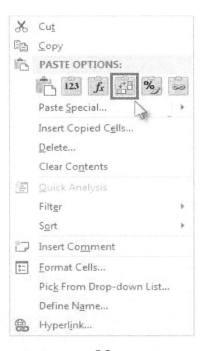

To select the data you want to rearrange and any column or row labels, press **Ctrl+C**.

By choosing a new place for the transposed table in the worksheet, you can ensure enough space for your data to be pasted. The new table you enter will replace any information or formatting in the current one.

To paste a transposed table, just right-click on the cell and choose **Transpose** from the context menu.

3.14 Data validation of cells

- Select the cell or cells for which you want to create a rule.
- Select Data Validation from the drop-down menu after selecting Data.

Choose Allow from the list of options on the Settings tab.

- **Whole Number** – for restricting the cell's acceptability to just whole numbers
- **Decimal** - for restricting the cell's acceptability to just decimal integers
- **List** - to choose data from a drop-down menu
- **Date** - for restricting the cell's acceptability to just dates

- **Time** - for restricting the cell's acceptance to just time
- **Text Length** - To restrict the text from becoming too long
- **Custom** – for the custom formula.

Choose the prerequisite under Data.

- Depending on the **Allow & Data** options you choose, provide the extra values that are required.
- Go to the **Input Message** page to customize the message that users will see while entering data.
- When the user selects or hovers over a cell, choose Show input data. When selecting a cell, tick the box to display the message (s).
- Select a **Style** from the **Error Alert** menu to customize your error message.
- Select **OK**.

An error alert with your message appears whenever the user tries to enter an incorrect value.

3.15 Flash Fill in Excel

Flash Fill automatically fills the data when it recognizes a pattern. For instance, you may separate the first and last name from a single column or combine the first and last name from two different columns using **Flash Complete**.

Windows / Mac OS

Imagine that initial names are in column A, last names are in column B, and combined first and last names are in column C. By typing your whole name into column C, you may instruct Excel's Flash Fill tool to fill in each of your columns according to a pattern you choose.

- The full name of the receiver should be entered in cell C2.
- Enter the whole name below in cell C3. Excel will show you a preview of the remaining column filled with the combined text if you provide it with a pattern.
- To accept the preview, press **ENTER**.

	A	B	C
1	First Name	Last Name	Full Name
2	Jay	Shasthri	Jay Shasthri
3	Pratap	Pillai	Pratap Pillai
4	Madhu	Srivastava	Madhu Srivastava
5	Victoria	Marsh	Victoria Marsh
6	David	Pizarro	David Pizarro

Flash Fill may not be enabled if you don't see a preview. Flash Fill may be performed manually by selecting Data, Flash Fill, or by hitting **Ctrl+E**. Make sure the "**Automatically Flash Fill**" checkbox is selected in the **Advanced Editing Options** submenu of the Tools menu.

3.16 Quick Analysis Tool in Microsoft Excel

Use the **Quick Analysis Tool** to see your data as a table or graphic.

Selecting the cells you want to investigate will help you analyze the data.

B
Listing Price
123,000
150,000
95,000
119,000
143,000

At the bottom of the results is an icon for the **Quick Analysis Tool** that should be noticed. It is merely only a few clicks.

	B	C
	Listing Price	**Town**
2	123,000	Camillu
8	150,000	Camillu
14	95,000	Camillu
20	119,000	Camillu
26	143,000	Camillu

Swiping your cursor over the thumbnail in the **Quick Analysis** gallery will allow you to preview each option.

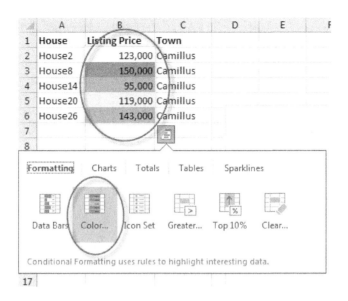

- Simply click an option to choose it.

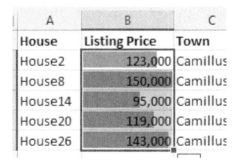

Chapter 4: Date Sorting (Data Organizing)

There is also a technique to do this. Many of Excel's sorting features may be unknown to you. Let's examine them one at a time, beginning with the fundamentals.

4.1 How to Sort in Excel

- Select the columns and rows you want to order.
- Select "**Sort**" from the "**Data**" drop-down menu at the top.
- Select the column you wish to use to lay out the document when sorting by columns.
- To filter by lines, choose "**Sort left-right**" from the "**Options**" menu.
- Select the items that you want to sort.
- Select the layout you want for your sheet.
- You should choose "**OK**."

The first series of instructions assume that you will use Microsoft Excel on a Mac. But don't worry; despite some differences in button placement, most earlier Excel versions' icons and available choices are still the same.

4.2 Highlight the Rows and Columns You Want to Be Sorted

In Excel, you may sort a group of cells by selecting and dragging the mouse over the spreadsheet to highlight all the cells you wish to sort, even those in columns and rows whose values through which you aren't sorting.

Ensure that the values in the B and C columns match the cells you are sorting in the A column; you must highlight these three columns if you try to sort the A column but find that the data in the B and C columns are aligned with the A column.

By examining the Harry Potter characters' last names in the figure below, you may see how to condense the sheet. However, the last name must be sorted, and the first name of everyone must match; otherwise, the sorted columns will not match.

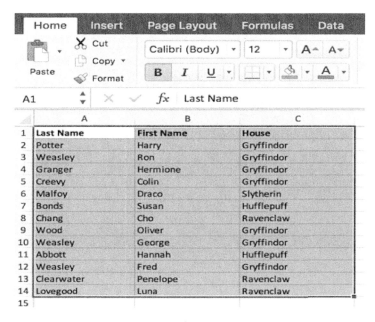

4.3 Navigate Toward 'Data' Along the Top & Select 'Sort'

The navigation pane's **"Data"** option should be selected after highlighting all the elements you wish to sort. Under this tab, the **"Sort"** button will show up, providing a new range of possibilities. You'll be eager to make purchases in directions other than alphabetically since the sign has an **"A-Z"** designation, as shown in the image below.

4.4 If You Are Sorting by The Column, Select That Column You Wish to Order the Sheet

As shown above, the **"Sort"** tab will provide a panel of alternatives for you. This is where you would list the items that need to be sorted and how they should be sorted.

Go to the "Column" dropdown menu on the left and choose the column whose contents you wish to use as sorting criteria if you want to filter by a category. The "Last Name" will be used in the following situation.

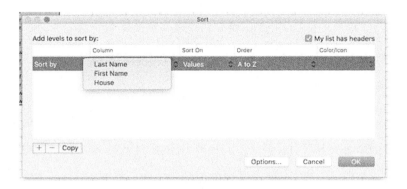

4.5 If You Are Sorting by The Row, Click The "Options" Icon & Select The "Sort Left to Right" Icon

Select "**Sort left-right**" from the "**Options**" menu item at the bottom if you'd rather sort by a single row than a column. Following that, a box for setting up the sort would reload, enabling you to choose the same "**Row**" from the leftmost dropdown menu (where it says "**Column**").

You will continue to sort by "**Last Name**" columns as this method of sorting is incorrect.

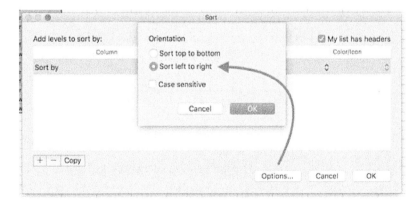

4.6 Choose What You'd Like Sorted

The contents of every cell need not be read thoroughly. The center column of the Sort options panel has the "**Sort On**" selection menu. The spreadsheet will sort by various attributes of each cell in the row or column you are sorting by when you click it. Cell color, font color, and any cell symbol are available options.

4.7 Choose How You'd Like to Order Your Sheet

There is an "**Order**" dropdown bar in the third section of the Sort options window. You may choose how you want the spreadsheet set up by selecting it.

The Sort options window's default recommendation is to sort alphabetically. You may also use a custom list or sort from A to Z. You may filter your data immediately, even before you finish creating your chart, by utilizing a few pre-made lists. You'll discover how and why you may sort by a custom list in the next few minutes.

4.8 To Sort by Number

You may even filter the spreadsheet by numbers if it has a number column in place of a letter-based data column. Choose this column from the "**Column**" selection menu on the left to do this. It will then be possible to choose "**Largest - Smallest**" or "**Smallest - Largest**" from the "**Order**" drop-down menu bar, respectively.

4.9 Click "Ok"

Once you click "**OK**" in the Sort options box, the list should be sorted following your criteria. Your Harry Potter page now displays, with last names listed alphabetically:

	A	B	C
1	Last Name	First Name	House
2	Abbott	Hannah	Hufflepuff
3	Bonds	Susan	Hufflepuff
4	Chang	Cho	Ravenclaw
5	Clearwater	Penelope	Ravenclaw
6	Creevy	Colin	Gryffindor
7	Granger	Hermione	Gryffindor
8	Lovegood	Luna	Ravenclaw
9	Malfoy	Draco	Slytherin
10	Potter	Harry	Gryffindor
11	Weasley	Ron	Gryffindor
12	Weasley	George	Gryffindor
13	Weasley	Fred	Gryffindor
14	Wood	Oliver	Gryffindor

4.10 How to Alphabetize in Excel?

Excel will alphabetize a cell in the column you wish to sort, allowing you to choose that cell. You may choose to sort in forward or reverse alphabetical order by going to the Data tab in the top menu. The sheet will be sorted by the column of the first highlighted cell if you click any of the tabs.

A data set that hasn't been organized may be encountered. A list of blog posts from marketing contacts may have been exported.

Whatever the circumstance, you may wish to begin by alphabetizing your list. A simple way to do this doesn't need any of the steps.

- Select any cell in a column to sort it.
- From the toolbar, choose the "**Data**" tab. Options for sorting are in the center.
- Next to the term "**Sort**," choose the left-side icon. Check the "**My set includes headers**" box in the pop-up if you have headers. Use the "**Cancel**" button if such is the situation.
- Select the icon with a downward-pointing cursor and the letters "**A**" and "**Z**" on top and bottom, respectively. The chart will then be arranged alphabetically from "**A**" to "**Z**." Click the icon with "**Z**" at the top and "**A**" at the bottom to arrange your chart in reverse alphabetical order.

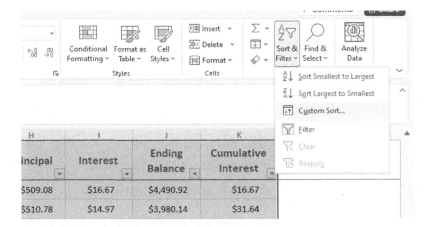

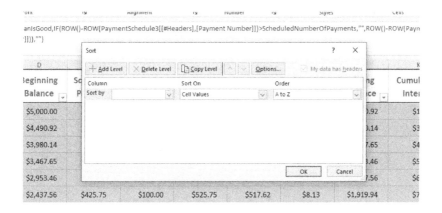

anIsGood,IF(ROW()-ROW(PaymentSchedule3[[#Headers],[Payment Number]])>ScheduledNumberOfPayments,"",ROW()-ROW(Payn
:]])),""}

4.11 Sorting Multiple Columns

You often want to sort two columns instead than simply one. Using a spreadsheet, let's say you want to organize all your blog posts by month before sorting them by blog post title or URL.

In this case, you should order the list by house number before sorting by the last name. You will get a chart that has been divided into each house and is alphabetized inside each house.

- To organize the information into a list, click on it.
- From the toolbar, choose the "**Data**" tab. Options for "**Sort**" may be found in the center.
- You should choose the icon to the left of the word "**Type**." The screen would show a pop-up window. If you have column headers, please make sure "The data include headers" is enabled.
- Three columns will be present. Select the first column you wish to sort by from the "**Column**" dropdown menu. (In this case, the word is "House.")

- Then click **"Add Level"** in the pop-up window's top left corner. Select **"Last-Name"** from the dropdown option under "Column."

- Make sure the table's **"Order"** column is set to A-Z. Next, click **"OK."**

- Your to-do list is well organized, which you appreciate.

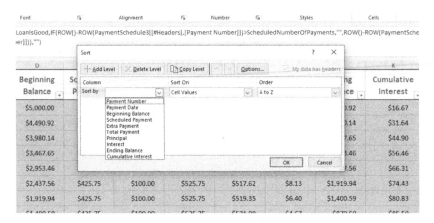

4.12 Sorting in Custom Order

Sorting from A to Z or Z to A is not your favorite. You can sometimes desire to sift through anything other than the weeks, months, or another organizing system.

In certain cases, you may be able to construct a bespoke order and specify exactly the kind of layout you desire. (It takes a course that resembles several columns but differs.)

Assume you know the month of everyone's birthday at Hogwarts and wish to organize the students by Birthday Month first, House second, and Last Name third.

- To sort your data in that column, click on a column heading.
- From the toolbar, choose the "**Data**" tab. The middle selections are "sort" options.
- You should choose the icon to the left of the word "**Type**." Check to see whether you have headers by double-clicking "The list has headers," which will appear in a pop-up window.
- Three columns will be present. Select the first column you wish to sort in the "**Column**" menu. It is, in this instance, "**Birthday Month**."
- Tap the dropdown next to "**A-Z**" in the "**Order**" tab. Select "**Custom List**" in the drop-down box.
- A few choices (month and day) and the chance to personalize your purchase are available. Select a month list with spelled-out months since this is consistent with the results. You should choose "**OK**" as your selection.
- the pop-up menu in the top left, and then choose "**Add Level**." Select "**House**" from the drop-down option under "**Column**."
- In a pop-up box, click the "**Add Level**" icon in the top left corner. Select "**Last-Name**" from the dropdown option under "**Column**."
- Make sure "House" and "**Last Name**" are in the "Order" column and are from A-Z. Next, click "**OK**."
- Your to-do list is well organized, which you appreciate.

nlsGood,IF(ROW()-ROW(PaymentSchedule3[[#Headers],[Payment Number]])>ScheduledNumberOfPayments,"",ROW()-ROW(PaymentSchedu
l)),"")

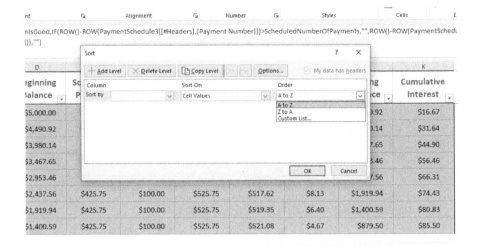

4.13 Sorting A Row

Your data may sometimes show in rows rather than columns. You will always sort the data in a slightly different step if this occurs.

- You may choose the data you wish to sort by clicking on a row.
- From the toolbar, choose the "**Data**" tab. The options for "**sort**" are in the center.
- Next to the term "**Sort**," choose the left-side icon. The screen would show a pop-up window.
- At the bottom of the page, choose "**Options**."
- Select "**Sort left-right**" under "Orientation." Next, click "**OK.**"
- Three columns will be present. Select the row number you wish to sort by from the "**Row**" option. (In this case, it is the first row.) Click "**OK**" when you're done.

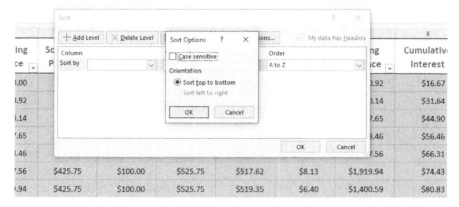

							K
ing	Sc					ng	Cumulativ
ce	P					ice	Interest
).00						).92	$16.67
).92						).14	$31.64
).14						7.65	$44.90
'.65						3.46	$56.46
1.46						7.56	$66.31
'.56	$425.75	$100.00	$525.75	$517.62	$8.13	$1,919.94	$74.43
1.94	$425.75	$100.00	$525.75	$519.35	$6.40	$1,400.59	$80.83

4.14 Sort Your Conditional Formatting

You'll sort by whether you use conditional formatting to change the color of a cell, including a symbol, or change the font colors.

In the diagram below, various colors have been used to symbolize various grade levels: The cell is green if they have a score of 90 or above. Yellow may be found between 80 and 90 degrees.

It becomes crimson at around 80 degrees. The information would be arranged so that the best performers are at the top. This data should be arranged such that the best performers are at the top.

- You may choose a row in which to organize your data by clicking on it.
- From the toolbar, choose the **"Data"** tab. The middle selections are **"sort"** options.

- Next to the term "**Sort**," choose the left-side icon. A pop-up box would read: Check to see whether "**The list has headers**" is selected.
- Three columns will be present. Select the first column you wish to sort by from the "**Column**" drop-down menu. It is "**Grades**" in this instance.
- From the "**Sort On**" column, choose "**Cell Color**."
- Click the green bar in the last column's "**Order**" box.
- Go to the drop-down menu and choose "**Add Level**." You may repeat steps 4-5 if required. Select the yellow bar rather than the green one under "**Order**."
- Select "**Add Level**" once. You may repeat steps 4-5 if required. Select the red bar under "**Order**" instead of the yellow bar.
- You should choose "**OK**."

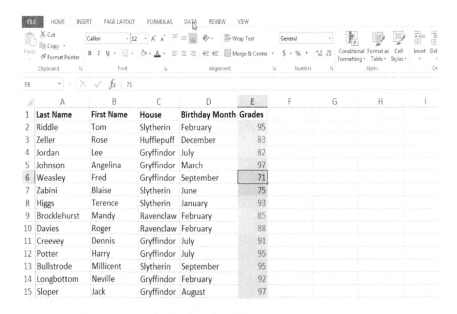

That is all Excel offers in terms of sorting. Are you preparing to set up the following spreadsheet? Start by downloading one of the nine Excel templates below, then arrange your data using Excel's sorting feature.

4.15 Filter

If you only want to see papers that meet certain criteria, you may filter the Excel files.

- Click on a cell in a data collection to select it.
- Select **Filter** from the **Sort & Filter group** on the **Data** screen.

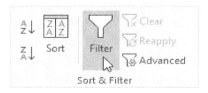

- The column heads include arrows.

	A	B	C	D	E
1	Last Nan ▼	Sales ▼	Count ▼	Quart ▼	
2	Smith	$16,753.00	UK	Qtr 3	
3	Johnson	$14,808.00	USA	Qtr 4	
4	Williams	$10,644.00	UK	Qtr 2	
5	Jones	$1,390.00	USA	Qtr 3	
6	Brown	$4,865.00	USA	Qtr 4	
7	Williams	$12,438.00	UK	Qtr 1	
8	Johnson	$9,339.00	UK	Qtr 2	
9	Smith	$18,919.00	USA	Qtr 3	
10	Jones	$9,213.00	USA	Qtr 4	
11	Jones	$7,433.00	UK	Qtr 1	
12	Brown	$3,255.00	USA	Qtr 2	
13	Williams	$14,867.00	USA	Qtr 3	
14	Williams	$19,302.00	UK	Qtr 4	
15	Smith	$9,698.00	USA	Qtr 1	
16					

- To select a nation, click the arrow next to it.
- To remove all checkboxes, click **Select All** and choose a checkbox next to the **USA**.

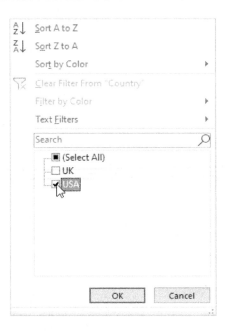

- Choose the **OK** option.
- Excel, therefore, only shows US-based revenue.

	A	B	C	D	E
1	Last Nan ▼	Sales ▼	Count ▼	Quart ▼	
3	Johnson	$14,808.00	USA	Qtr 4	
5	Jones	$1,390.00	USA	Qtr 3	
6	Brown	$4,865.00	USA	Qtr 4	
9	Smith	$18,919.00	USA	Qtr 3	
10	Jones	$9,213.00	USA	Qtr 4	
12	Brown	$3,255.00	USA	Qtr 2	
13	Williams	$14,867.00	USA	Qtr 3	
15	Smith	$9,698.00	USA	Qtr 1	
16					

- To choose a **Quarter**, press the arrow next to it.
- To remove all checkboxes, select all and then click the check box next to **Qtr 4**.

- From the drop-down option, choose **OK**.
- Excel thus only shows income for Quarter 4 for the United States.

	A	B	C	D	E
1	Last Nan ▾	Sales ▾	Count ▾	Quart ▾	
3	Johnson	$14,808.00	USA	Qtr 4	
6	Brown	$4,865.00	USA	Qtr 4	
10	Jones	$9,213.00	USA	Qtr 4	
16					

- To remove the filter from the **Sort & Filter** group on the **Data** page, click the **Clear** button. Select **Filter** to get rid of the filter and the arrows.

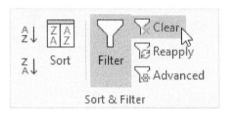

- Excel data needs to be filtered more quickly.
- Choose a cell from the list.

	A	B	C	D	E
1	Last Name	Sales	Country	Quarter	
2	Smith	$16,753.00	UK	Qtr 3	
3	Johnson	$14,808.00	USA	Qtr 4	
4	Williams	$10,644.00	UK	Qtr 2	
5	Jones	$1,390.00	USA	Qtr 3	
6	Brown	$4,865.00	USA	Qtr 4	
7	Williams	$12,438.00	UK	Qtr 1	
8	Johnson	$9,339.00	UK	Qtr 2	
9	Smith	$18,919.00	USA	Qtr 3	
10	Jones	$9,213.00	USA	Qtr 4	
11	Jones	$7,433.00	UK	Qtr 1	
12	Brown	$3,255.00	USA	Qtr 2	
13	Williams	$14,867.00	USA	Qtr 3	
14	Williams	$19,302.00	UK	Qtr 4	
15	Smith	$9,698.00	USA	Qtr 1	
16					

- Select **Filter** and right-click on the context menu to select **Filter by Selected Cell's Value**.

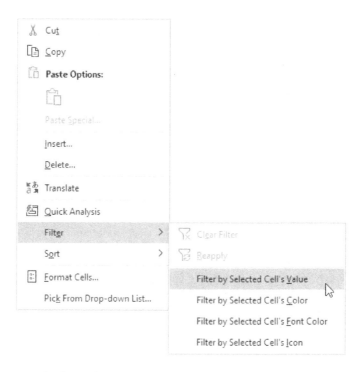

- Excel, therefore, only shows US-based revenue.

	A	B	C	D	E
1	Last Nan ▾	Sales ▾	Count ▾	Quart ▾	
3	Johnson	$14,808.00	USA	Qtr 4	
5	Jones	$1,390.00	USA	Qtr 3	
6	Brown	$4,865.00	USA	Qtr 4	
9	Smith	$18,919.00	USA	Qtr 3	
10	Jones	$9,213.00	USA	Qtr 4	
12	Brown	$3,255.00	USA	Qtr 2	
13	Williams	$14,867.00	USA	Qtr 3	
15	Smith	$9,698.00	USA	Qtr 1	
16					

- To further sort this data collection, choose a different cell from a different column.

Chapter 5: Tables and Charts in Excel

Visual representations of information, regardless of subject matter, facilitate understanding. Numbers that need to be compared benefit greatly from this. Graphs are the best choice of representation here. Excel will be your main tool.

In addition, you'll pick up the skills to make dynamic graphs and charts that refresh themselves as the underlying data is modified.

5.1 What is an Excel Table?

Excel is a spreadsheet program that gives you many options. Tables are used to store the data you enter. Tables let Excel know that all the data it receives is related. The sole factor that connects the data without needing a table is their proximity.

If you create your tables in Excel, you can evaluate the data more quickly. To create a structured table from a list of data, use the table order. Use Excel Table's sorting and filtering features to make the data more structured and ordered. Additionally, tables may easily be updated using formulae.

Follow the guidelines below to arrange the data before generating a prepared Table.

- The data must be arranged in rows and columns.
- Each column in the first row needs a header.
- There must be just one piece of information in each column.

- There cannot be any empty rows or columns in the list.

What configuration of the table works best?

- To make a table, select every data list in the worksheet.

- On the **Insert** tab, choose **Table** from the **Tables** category.

- The **Create Table** dialogue box allows you to choose the data range.

- Your "perceived" range is adjustable in the **Create Table** dialogue box. Therefore, choose the checkbox next to **"My table has headers"** and press **OK**.

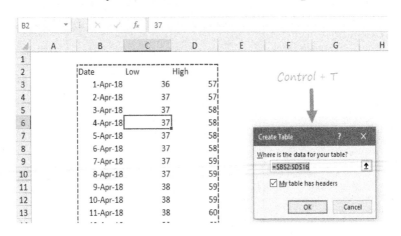

- After that, the data is turned into Excel tables.

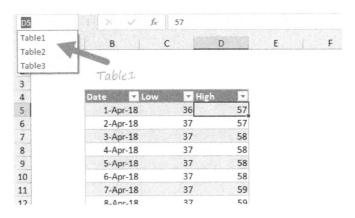

Table Sorting

These basic procedures will help you sort the data in a table:

- Select **Sort A to Z** from the arrow next to the item's name.
- Then press the **OK** button.

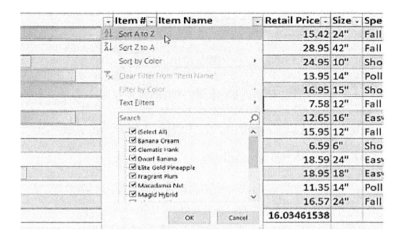

Table Filtering

By following these easy steps, you may pick how to order your Table or whatever data you want to see:

- Select **Specialty** by selecting the arrow next to **Category**.
- Then press the **OK** button.

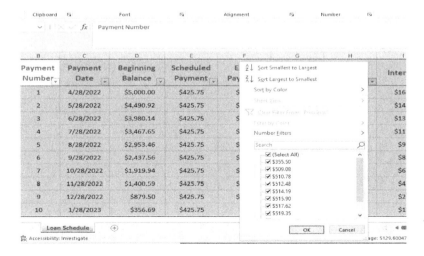

5.2 Making Pivot Table and Charts

You'll learn how to create pivot tables and charts in this part.

Having access to the pivot table is crucial.

A useful tool for condensing, arranging, sorting, and analyzing data in a table is the pivot table.

The steps for creating a pivot table are as follows:

- Decide which cell will serve as the basis for your pivot table.
- Select **Pivot Table** from the **Insert** page.

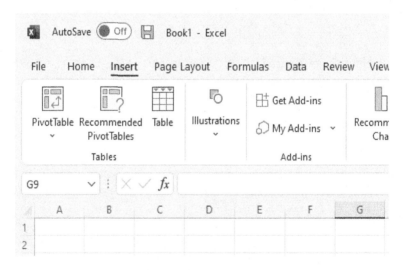

- A table or a range of data may be evaluated, so make your choice.
- When asked, "**Choose where you want the Pivot Table to be placed**," choose either the **New worksheet** or **Existing worksheet**.
- Next, click the **OK** button.

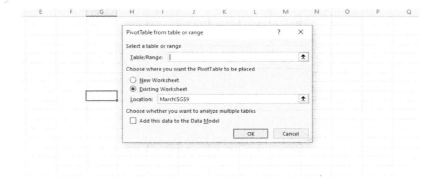

- Go to the **Pivot Tables** pane and select the field name checkbox to add a field to a pivot table.

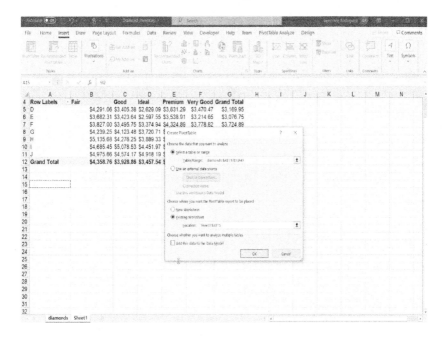

- Simply drag the field to the desired spot using your mouse if you want to modify its position.

Your table should be like the one below if you followed the procedures above.

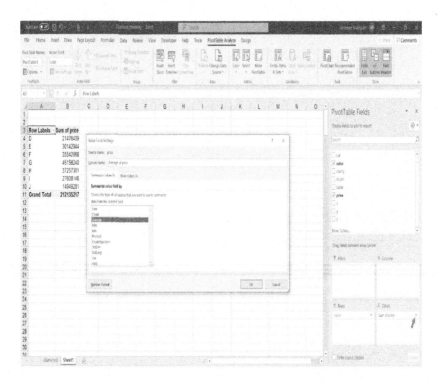

The Pivot Chart

The results from the pivot table are shown graphically in the pivot chart.

The procedures listed below may be used to produce a pivot chart from a pivot table:

- Pick the desired pivot table cell.
- **Pivot Chart** should be selected from the **Insert** menu.
- Then press the **OK** button.

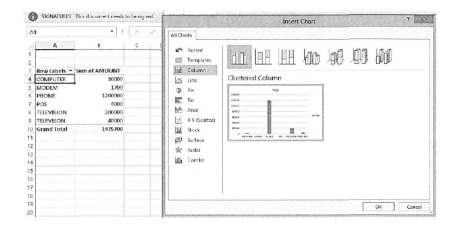

Your pivot table and chart should appear like the one below if you followed the guidelines above.

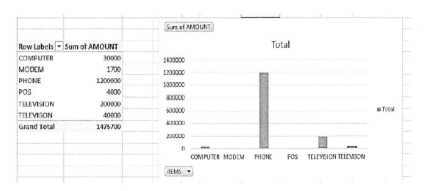

Use of Slicer on Pivot Table

Use the slicer tool to filter the data on tables or Pivot tables. The results may be sorted using a button on the Excel spreadsheet.

- Select each cell in the **Table** or **Pivot table** to use **Slicer**.
- Slicer may be found under **Insert** on the **Home** page.
- Choose the area you wish to see from the **Insert Slicers** dialogue box checkboxes.

- Then press the **OK** button.

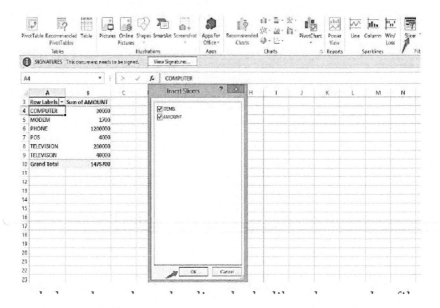

This is how the Slicer appears when sorting data on a server or in a pivot table.

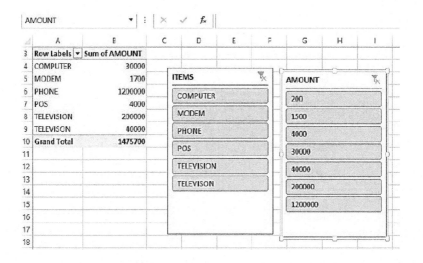

5.3 Working with Charts

Excel charts enable you to visually evaluate the data on your worksheet by displaying it as rows and columns of bars on a chart. There are many different types of charts that may be used to display results. Just a few of the charts Excel offers include a pie chart, a line chart, a bar chart, and a column chart.

Charted data is more engaging, audible, and easier to read and comprehend. You will examine the data and find discrepancies between various values using charts.

5.4 Types of Excel Charts

Excel has many different types of charts, but we will briefly go through a few of them.

Column Charts

In this graph, the horizontal axis divisions contrast with the vertical axis. There are several varieties of column charts, including stacked columns, clustered columns, 3-D stacked columns, and more.

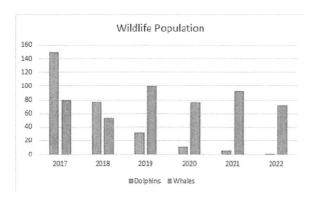

Line Chart

This graph shows data trends across various periods, such as months, years, days, etc. More line maps are available, including line stacks with arrows and 100% stacks.

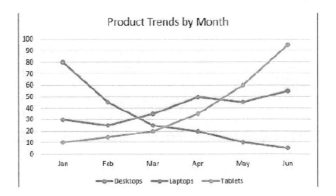

Bar Chart

Like a column chart, a bar chart connects horizontal axis groups to vertical axis data. There are many kinds of styles. For big-label messaging, the bar map is used. Examples of bar charts include clustered, stacked, three-dimensional, and other types.

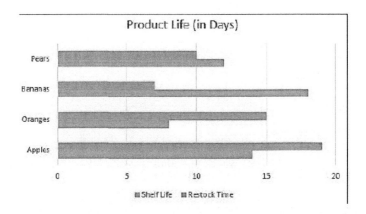

Pie Chart

It is a graph that uses a circular graph to illustrate or describe results. This graph uses a pie slice design to show data and specifics.

Doughnut Chart

It's a graph that illustrates how parts relate to the whole, and much like a pie chart, when all the pieces are added together, the result is 100%. In contrast to the pie chart, which can only hold one data series, the doughnut pie chart can store many data series.

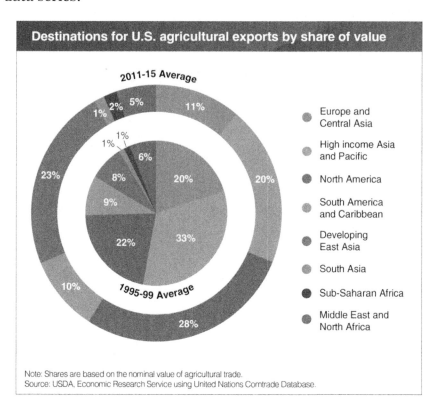

Note: Shares are based on the nominal value of agricultural trade.
Source: USDA, Economic Research Service using United Nations Comtrade Database.

123

5.5 How to Insert Chart in Excel?

- Select the information for the chart.

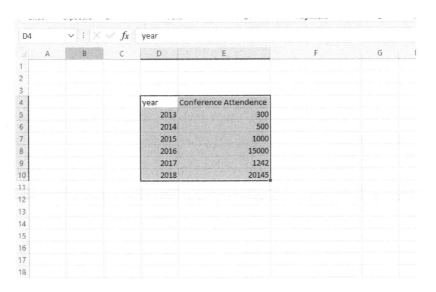

- Click **Recommended Charts** from the drop-down option and then select **Insert**.

- From the list of suggested charts, choose a chart to see.

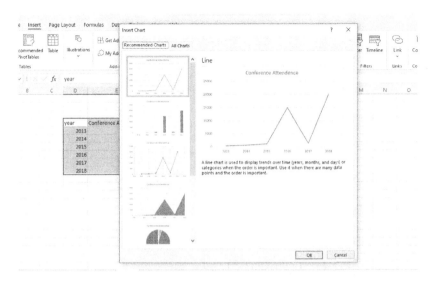

- Once you've decided on the **Chart**, click the **OK** button.

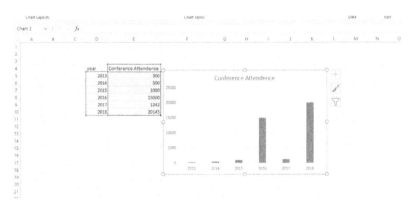

Giving a title to Chart

Anybody taking a quick look at your Excel spreadsheet will be able to recognize or remember the purpose of the Chart after giving it a name. Do the following to give your Chart a title:

- Anywhere on the chart area may be clicked.

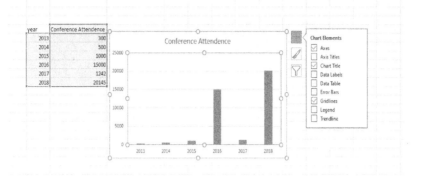

- In the upper right corner of the **Table**, click the **addition** icon.

- Then, from all the available options, choose the Chart title.

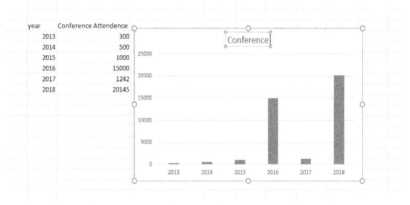

- To switch from **Chart Title** to another title, just click inside the textbox.

5.6 Changing Chart Type in Excel

The many chart types used in data visualization are numerous. Change to a different chart that more accurately represents your data if the format you chose for the chart to display your data is not suitable or necessary.

To complete this assignment, follow these steps:

- You may update a chart by clicking on it.

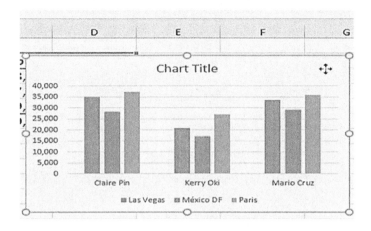

- The **Design** tab's **Change Chart Type** option is available.

- When you select **Change Chart Type**, a slider box enabling you to choose between **Suggested charts** or **All charts** will appear.

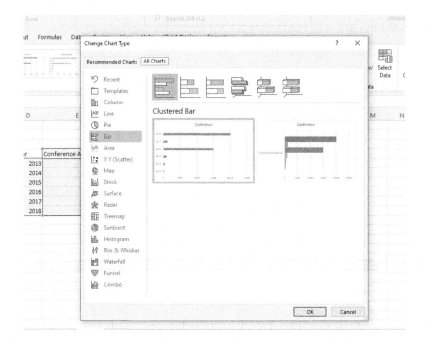

- You may get a preview of any chart.

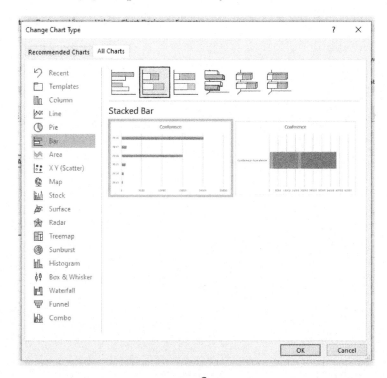

- The Chart will appear on the worksheet after you click **"OK."**

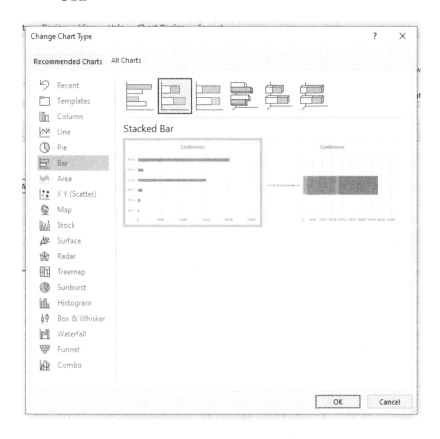

5.7 Change Style of Chart in Excel

To change the chart type in an Excel spreadsheet, follow these steps:

- You can modify the chart by clicking on it, and you may make changes.

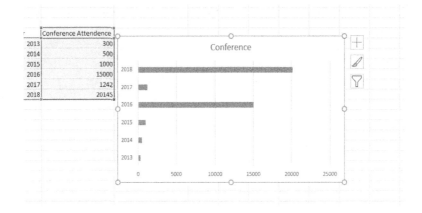

- Select **Change Chart Style** from the **Design** page.

- The chart type will be modified on this page.

5.8 Changing Chart Layout

- You may update a chart by clicking on it.

- You may update a chart by clicking on the one you want to edit.
- Choose the chart type you want, and the modifications will appear in the chart.

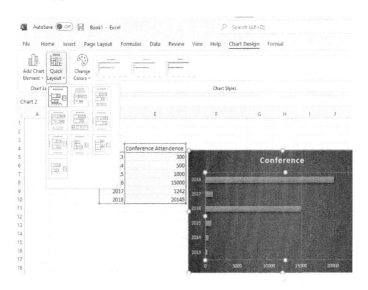

5.9 Switching Rows & Columns in Chart

It would make it easier to customize the rows and columns of the data in charts to meet your needs.

- To do this, click on the **Chart** you want to change and then select it.

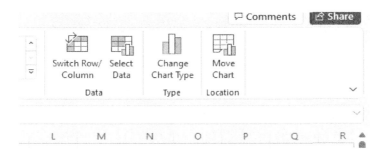

- The **Design** tab's **Switch Row/Column** option is available.
- This tab will adjust the rows and columns of the details.

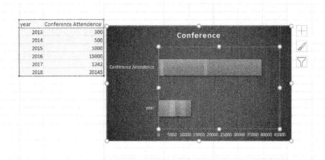

Moving a Chart

A chart may be moved from any place on an existing worksheet to a new or existing worksheet.

Drag a chart to the desired location inside a worksheet using the mouse but click and drag it to another worksheet to move it there.

You may update a chart by clicking on it.

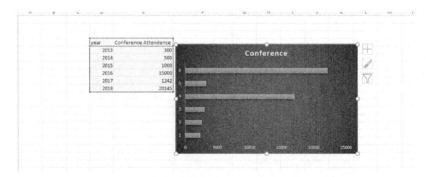

- The **Design** tab's **Move Chart Location** option is available.

- A window will pop up once you click the **Move Chart Location** button, enabling you to choose the location where you want the **Chart** to be displayed.

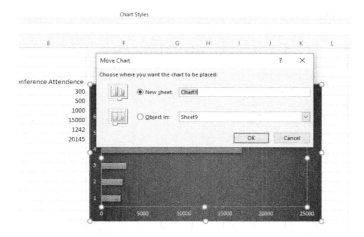

- The Chart will be moved to another worksheet after you click "**OK**."

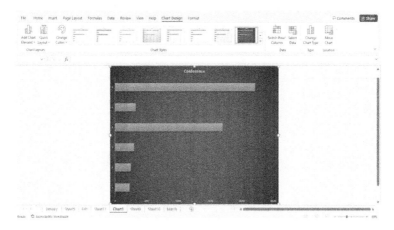

5.10 Resizing a Chart

Depending on your needs, you may alter a map's size to be too little or too large. These individuals will do this procedure:

- When you click on the map to make it updated, some loop handles could appear around the edges.
- The loop handles may be used to reposition the Chart's horizontal and vertical alignment.

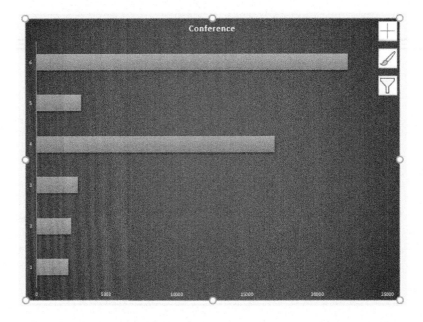

- You may alter the chart's scale by clicking on the loop handles.

Chapter 6: Excel Mathematical Functions

If you've come this far in your quest to learn more about Excel, regardless of how experienced an Excel user you are or how unfamiliar you are, there are a few formulas and functions you should be familiar with.

As a result, you'll take your time studying the fundamental equations and operations you'll need.

6.1 Mathematical Function

Math functions are used for numerical tasks, including addition, calculating percentages of totals, and basic financial analysis.

6.2 Sum Function

The values of many rows or columns may be added or summed using the SUM function.

=SUM (num 1, [num 2]).

Follow these procedures to use the SUM function.

- Create the SUM feature in the cell.
- To choose cells for the cell range box, go to the Function argument.
- Press the **Enter** key after that.

The SUM function accepts the following inputs.

The function accepts the following arguments:

- **Number1:** This is the first numeric value to be added.
- **Number2:** This is the second numeric value to be added.

Let's use the table and the Aggregate function to get the total revenue from Monday through Friday.

	A	B	C	D	E	F
1						
2						
3						
4						
5		Days of Week	Sales			
6		Monday	15000			
7		Tuesday	21400			
8		Wednesday	24541			
9		Thursday	6521			
10		Friday	15474			
11		Saturday	13574			
12		Sunday	15424			

E13

The techniques below may be used to monitor revenue from Monday through Friday using Total.

Put the feature with the cell set in an empty cell filled in as follows: **=SUM (A2:B6).**

SUM   ⌄ ⋮ ✕ ✓ *fx*   =Sum(C6:C12)

	A	B	C	D	E	F
1						
2						
3						
4						
5		Days of Week	Sales			
6		Monday	15000			
7		Tuesday	21400			
8		Wednesday	24541			
9		Thursday	6521			
10		Friday	15474			
11		Saturday	13574			
12		Sunday	15424			
13						
14		Total Sale	=Sum(C6:C12)			
15						
16						

If the conditions mentioned above were satisfied, your weekly net income would be **113327**.

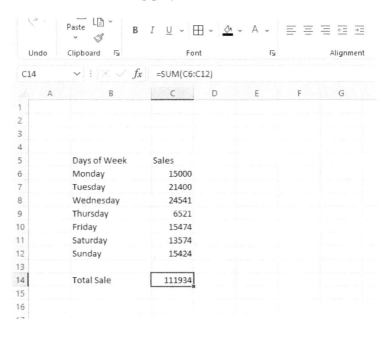

	A	B	C	D	E	F	G
1							
2							
3							
4							
5		Days of Week	Sales				
6		Monday	15000				
7		Tuesday	21400				
8		Wednesday	24541				
9		Thursday	6521				
10		Friday	15474				
11		Saturday	13574				
12		Sunday	15424				
13							
14		Total Sale	111934				
15							
16							

C14   ⌄ ⋮ ✕ ✓ *fx*   =SUM(C6:C12)

When using the SUM function, keep this in mind.

- A value error occurs if the criteria are more than 255 characters.
- The SUM function instantly disqualifies empty cell types with text values.
- Constants, sets, named ranges, and cell references are acceptable parameters.
- The SUM function returns an error for each incorrect statement.

6.3 SUMIF Function

To sum up, the SUM function uses a collection of arguments, the cells.

Dates, numbers, and words create the criterion or requirements.

Additionally, this work employs wildcards (*,) and logical operators like >.

The following inputs are used with the SUMIF technique.

=SUMIF (range, criteria, [sum_range]

Range (Mandatory Argument): The number of cells that the expanded criterion may be applied to.

Criteria: It establishes which cells may be concatenated (Required Argument). There are several methods to offer criteria arguments.

- Numbers, integers, and times are examples of numerical values.
- Terms like Monday, East, Price, and others may be found in text strings.
- Examples of expressions are the phrases >11 and 3.

Sum range (Optional Argument): If there are more cells to sum than those specified in the range argument, this cell must be added.

Application of SUMIF

Let's check whether the US and January revenue calculations are done using the SUMIF function.

	A	B	C	D
			f_x	
B10				
	A	B	C	D
1	MONTH	COUNTRY	SALES	
2	JAN	USA	23,000	
3	FEB	ENGLAND	12,990	
4	JAN	USA	12,987	
5	MARCH	FRANCE	32,200	
6	JAN	ITALY	32,150	
7	FEB	USA	33,212	
8	JAN	USA	12,900	

First, use the methods below to determine how much money you made in January.

- Leave the role blank to ensure that the cell set is rounded up. **SUM (A2:A8)**.
- Fill in the gaps for January's requirements. **SUM (JAN, A2:A8,)**.

139

- The information below shows that 81,037 sales were made in January.

To determine the overall number of sales made in the US.

- Fill the role with the cell set to be summed by typing **=SUM** into an empty cell **(B2:B8).**

| C10 | ⌄ | ⋮ | ✕ | ✓ | f_x | =SUMIF(A2:A8, "Jan", C2:C8) |

	A	B	C	D	E	F	G	H	I	J
1	Month	Country								
2	Jan	USA	23000							
3	Feb	England	12900							
4	Jan	USA	12987							
5	March	France	32200							
6	Jan	Italy	32150							
7	Feb	USA	33212							
8	Jan	USA	12900							
9										
10	Total Sales		81037							
11										
12										
13										
14										

The table below displays the gross sales in the United States.

| C10 | ⌄ | ⋮ | ✕ | ✓ | f_x | =SUMIF(B2:B8, "USA", C2:C8) |

	A	B	C	D	E	F
1	Month	Country				
2	Jan	USA	23000			
3	Feb	England	12900			
4	Jan	USA	12987			
5	March	France	32200			
6	Jan	Italy	32150			
7	Feb	USA	33212			
8	Jan	USA	12900			
9						
10	Total Sales		82099			
11						
12						

When using the SUMIF FUNCTION, keep this in mind.

- If the provided criteria are longer than 255 characters, a VALUE! An error will appear.
- Due to the absence of a defined total range, the cells in the range would automatically be added.
- If you don't put double quotes around text strings in parameters, it won't fit.
- Those SUMIF function wildcards? Additionally, you may use the sign *.

6.4 The Role of SUMIFs

Cells that satisfy several requirements or conditions are grouped using the SUMIFS function. Times, numbers, and words create the criterion or requirements. This function uses wildcards (*?) and logical operators like>, etc.

Use of SUMIFS

Let's figure out how many apples the total Pete has provided in the table below using the SUMIFS function.

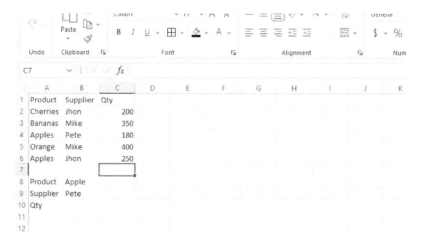

Use the steps listed below to determine how much Apple Pete supplies.

Fill up the part with the cell set to be summed up =**SUMIFS** in the empty cell (**C 2: C 6, A 2: A 6, "apples," B 2: B 6, "Pete"**).

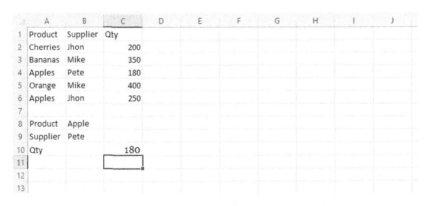

180 apples will be provided in total if your formula is followed.

	A	B	C	D	E	F	G	H	I	J
1	Product	Supplier	Qty							
2	Cherries	Jhon	200							
3	Bananas	Mike	350							
4	Apples	Pete	180							
5	Orange	Mike	400							
6	Apples	Jhon	250							
7										
8	Product	Apple								
9	Supplier	Pete								
10	Qty		180							
11										
12										
13										

When employing SUMIFS functionalities, you must adhere to the following requirements:

- Industry standards require text strings to be contained in double quotations ("), such as "orange."

- Similar rows and columns must be present in the additional range to a sum range.
- Instances when the specified ranges are not aligned result in a **#VALUE** error.
- Industry guidelines state that quotations don't include references to cells.
- SUMIFS should be used with ranges, not arrays.

6.5 MOD Function

When a sum (dividend) is divided by another integer, the MOD function is employed to determine what is left over (divisor).

The following parameters are used to invoke the MOD function:

- You need to find the remainder for that number. (Required presumption) (Required Argument) Dividend: The amount you want to split the total by.

Application of MOD Function

Use the MOD function to get the last cell A2 in the table below.

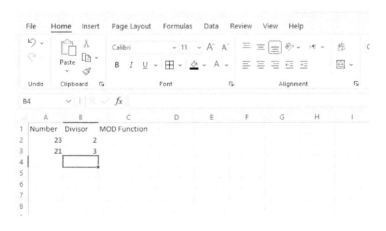

The actions below should be followed to find A2:

- In a blank cell, enter the function, the numbers, and the divisor =**MOD (A2, B2)**.

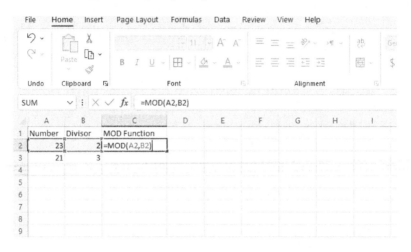

- The graphic below depicts the outcome of the previous step.

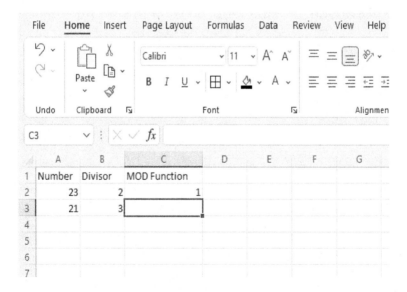

The following should be kept in mind while using the MOD function:

- #DID/o! If the divisor value is negative, there is a problem.
- The output of the MOD function will match the divisor's sign.

6.6 The RANDBETWEEN Function

Based on the input values, the RANDBETWEEN function outputs a random number. Every time the worksheet is accessed or edited; this feature is activated.

The following parameters are used when using the RANDBETWEEN function:

Down: This is the least integer in the set that the function may return (Mandatory Function).

Peak The greatest integer the function may produce in the set (Mandatory Function).

Application of RANDBETWEEN Function

Let's examine the table below to see how the RANDBETWEEN function is used.

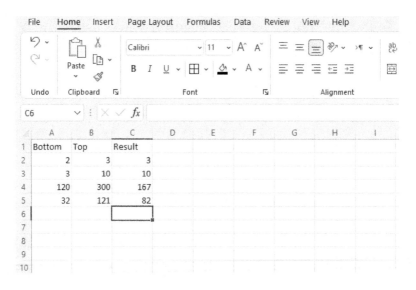

The table above uses the RANDBETWEEN method (A2, B2).

- The worksheet's outcome varies when the equations in the table are repeated, as seen below.

	A	B	C	D
1	Bottom	Top	Result	
2	2	3	2	
3	3	10	8	
4	120	300	181	
5	32	121	87	

=RANDBETWEEN(A2, B2)

There are a few things to consider while using the RANDBETWEEN tool.

- The worksheet is tabulated or updated when the RANDBETWEEN function produces a new value.

- Enter the RANDBETWEEN function in the formula bar and press F9 to transform the model into its output rather than changing the random number as the worksheet is generated.
- Select a cell, input the RANDBETWEEN module, then press Ctrl + Enter to produce a collection of random integers over several cells.

6.7 Round Function

The ROUND function, which increases a number's digit count, is what it is known as. Using this feature, you may round up or down. The arguments are used with the ROUND function.

Number 1 (Mandatory Argument): Round this number to the nearest whole number.

The amount should be rounded to these many digits. Several digits (Mandatory Argument): This is how many digits should be used to round the value.

Application of ROUND Function

Using the Circular function, round 1844.123 to one decimal place, two decimal places, closest number, nearest 10, nearest 100, and nearest 1000.

- Use **1844.123 =ROUND** to the closest decimal place (A1,1).

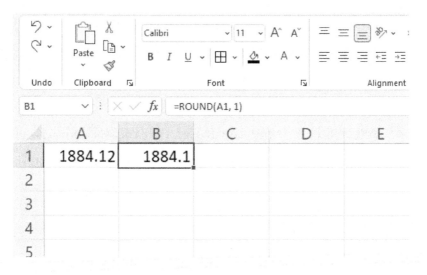

- Enter **1844.123 =ROUND** to round the number to the nearest whole number (A1, 0)

6.8 ROUNDDOWN Function

You may round numbers to a certain number of decimal places with the ROUND DOWN function.

The ROUND DOWN function uses the preceding inputs.

Rounding up is (number, num digits)

Number 1: Round down to the nearest whole number using this value (Mandatory Argument).

(Required Argument) several digits: The count of rounding numbers is this one.

Application of ROUNDDOWN

Using the ROUNDDOWN function, round up 1233.345 to the nearest integer, nearest 100, closest 1000, nearest two decimal places, and nearest number.

- Add one decimal point to **1233.345** to round it off. **=ROUNDDOWN (A1, 1)**

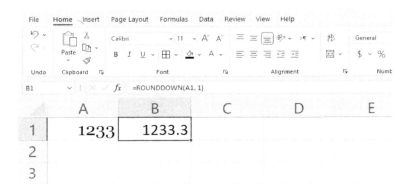

- Round up by **1233.345** to the nearest thousandths **(=ROUNDUP) (A1, -3)**

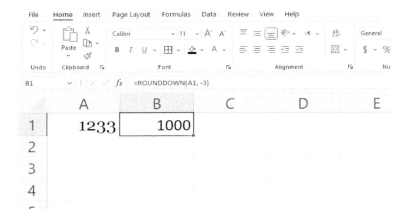

Sorting Function

The Sort function is used to arrange a column's output in either ascending or descending order.

The SORT function uses the statements.

=SORT (array, [sort_index], [sort_order], [by col])

Array (This justification is required.): This set or order of values will be omitted from further consideration.

Sort_index (Additional Argument): Which column or row should be sorted is specified.

Sort_order (Additional Argument): This number is used to sort the cells; 1 indicates ascending order, while -1 indicates downward order. The results will be sorted in ascending order if this part is omitted.

By col (Supplementary Argument): With FALSE indicating row filtering and TRUE implying column sorting, this determines the sorting direction.

Application of SORT Function

Sort the cells in the table below in ascending order using the SORT algorithm.

	A	B	C
1	Item	Qty.	
2	Apples	30	
3	Cherries	29	
4	Grapes	31	
5	Lemons	34	
6	Oranges	36	
7	Peachs	25	
8	Pears	40	
9			

Use the instructions below to sort the items in ascending order, starting with the lowest item, and working your way up.

- See what occurs by entering the function **(=SORT)**, the source array (A2:B8), the sort of index (2), and the sort order (1). Finally, the formula =**SORT (A2:B8, 2, 1)** will be typed by clicking on the empty cell.
- When you press **Enter**, the data will be analyzed in ascending order.

D1 | =SORT(A2:B8, 2, 1)

	A	B	C	D	E	F
1	Item	Qty.		Peachs	25	
2	Apples	30		Cherries	29	
3	Cherries	29		Apples	30	
4	Grapes	31		Grapes	31	
5	Lemons	34		Lemons	34	
6	Oranges	36		Oranges	36	
7	Peachs	25		Pears	40	
8	Pears	40				
9						

To set up in decreasing order, starting with the greatest value.

- You may insert the desired feature by clicking on an empty cell. The root list (A2:B8), sort of index (2), and sort order are all equivalent to SORT (1). Not to mention, **=SORT (A2:B8, 2, - 1)**.

- When you press **Enter**, the data will be arranged in ascending order.

D1 | =SORT(A2:B8, 2, -1)

	A	B	C	D	E	F
1	Item	Qty.		Pears	40	
2	Apples	30		Oranges	36	
3	Cherries	29		Lemons	34	
4	Grapes	31		Grapes	31	
5	Lemons	34		Apples	30	
6	Oranges	36		Cherries	29	
7	Peachs	25		Peachs	25	
8	Pears	40				
9						

Facts To Consider Regarding The SORT Function

- The SORT algorithm uses the first column as an example to sort things in ascending order.
- Microsoft 365 subscribers are the only ones who can use the SORT feature.
- When the source data is modified, the output is immediately updated.

Chapter 7: Excel Financial Functions

Numerous financial procedures are conducted using Excel's financial functions, including yield estimation, interest rate computation, internal rate of return computation, stock valuations, and asset depreciation. The features are included in Excel 2021 and later editions but are unavailable in older versions. Here is a list of Excel's financial features that are most often used:

7.1 PV Function

Using a fixed interest rate and debt or investment, the PV equation (Present Value) determines the present value of the obligation or investment. Mortgages and other investments that have recurring, periodic fees may be used with the PV function, or a projected value (investment objective) =**PV (rate, nper, pmt, [fv], [type])**.

	A	B	C
1			
2	Annual Interest Rate	3.50%	
3	Periodic Payment	500	
4	Number of Periods (Monthly)	72	
5	Compounding Periods per year	12	
6	Present Value		
7			
8			
9			

Using the PV function, determine the table's current value.

- Write the goal and the defense in a blank cell. (B2/B5, B4, B3, 0, 0) =PV

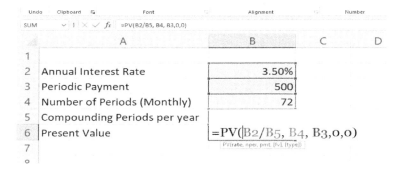

	A	B	C	D
1				
2	Annual Interest Rate	3.50%		
3	Periodic Payment	500		
4	Number of Periods (Monthly)	72		
5	Compounding Periods per year			
6	Present Value	=PV(B2/B5, B4, B3,0,0)		
7		PV(rate, nper, pmt, [fv], [type])		
8				

- When you press enter, the sum will be -£32,428.79, as shown in the table below.

7.2 FV Function

The prospective value of an investment or loan with a constant interest rate and recurring constant dividend is determined using the FV equation.

The FV function operates with the following inputs.

=FV (rate, nper, pmt, [pv], [type])

- **Rate (Necessary Argument)**: This is the interest rate for each compounding period.
- **Nper**: This is the entire amount of money spent throughout a person's lifetime.
- **Pmt (Supplementary Argument)**: The payment date is provided in the Pmt. If this defense is not made, the PV defense must be given.
- **PV (Supplementary Argument)**: This is the investment's or loan's current value. If the PV argument is not supplied, the Pmt parameter must be provided.

- **Type (Supplementary Argument)**: Indicates whether payments are paid at the beginning or end of the year.
- When one is entered, the payment period is at the beginning of the month; when zero is entered, it is after the term.

Use the FV function to determine the potential value of the table.

- Type **B3/B5, B4*B5, 0, -B2, =FV** in the blank field and enter your function name and parameter.

	Undo	Clipboard	🗔		Font		🗔		Alignment	
SUM		∨ ⋮ × ✓	*fx*	=FV(B3/B5, B4*B5,0, -B2)						
	A			B	C	D	E	F	G
1									
2	Present Value			20000					
3	Interest Rate			5%					
4	Term(Year)			14					
5	Compounding Period Per Year			12					
6	Future Value			=FV(B3/B5, B4*B5,0, -B2)					
7				FV(rate, nper, pmt, [pv], [type])					
8									
9									
10									

7.3 NPV Function

A calculation known as an NPV function uses a discount rate and several potential cash flows to determine an investment's net present value.

An NPV function accepts the following inputs.

(rate, value 1, [value 2]) = NPV

Rate (Necessary Argument): The lifetime discount rate is represented by this.

Value1 (Mandatory Argument): It represents the first payment or revenue in a series. Negative payments stand in for outgoing transactions, whereas positive payments signify receiving payments.

Value2 (Optional Argument): Its value displays many payments and sources of revenue to calculate the investment's net present value.

- Write the goal and the defense in a blank cell.

Undo	Clipboard	⌐		Font		⌐	Alignment		⌐	Number

SUM ˅ ⫶ ✕ ✓ *fx* =NPV(B9,B3:B8)

	A	B	C	D	E	F
2	Period	Cash Flow				
3		0	700			
4		1	200			
5		2	300			
6		3	400			
7		4	500			
8		5	600			
9	Required Return	15%				
10						
11	NPV	=NPV(B9,B3:B8)				
12		NPV(rate, value1, [value2], [value3], ...)				

SLN Function

Using a straight-line degradation mechanism, the SLN function helps compute an asset's depreciation over a single period.

To conduct its tasks, the SLN function receives the following inputs.

=SLN (cost, salvage, life)

Cost (Obligatory Argument): This represents the initial investment in a rescued item.

Salvage (Assumed Argument): This is the asset's value at the end of its useful life, sometimes referred to as its salvage value.

Life: The number of depreciations an asset experiences, often known as the object's useful life.

The part following will take depreciation into account.

- Write the function name and an argument into an empty cell.

= SLN (B 3, B 4, B 5)

Undo	Clippoara	ʁ		Font		ʁ	Alignmen

SUM		∨ : × ✓ fx	=SLN(B3,B4,B5)				
	A		B	SLN(cost, salvage, life)	E	F	G
2							
3	Cost of the Asset		55000				
4	Salvage Value		8500				
5	Useful Life		10				
6	SLN		=SLN(B3,B4,B5)				
7							
8							
9							

7.4 SYD Function

The SYD function is a technique for calculating how many years an asset will depreciate over a certain period. The asset's cost, salvage value, & the number of depreciations are considered by this function.

The SYD function accepts the following inputs for use in doing its work.

=SYD (cost, salvage, life, per)

Cost (obligatory argument): This is the initial price of the asset.

Salvage (Required Argument): This is the asset's salvage value or worth at the end of depletion.

Life (Obligatory Argument): The quantity of depreciation that occurs throughout an asset's useful life.

Per (Required Argument): The depreciation would be computed according to the period.

The total depreciation of the assets in the following table is calculated by summing the years of depreciation.

- Write the goal and the supporting evidence in the blank cell.

= SYD (B 2, B 3, B 4, B 5)

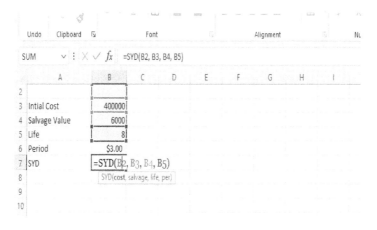

Chapter 8: Excel Logical Functions

Using logical functions may help you make decisions by helping you analyze a cell's contents, do a calculation, and then compare the outcome to the desired value. The logical function may also be used to show data and further calculate whether a condition is true or false. Examples include the logical operations IF, NOT, OR, IFS, and others.

8.1 IF Function

When a statement is true, the IF function, which is a check function, returns one value; when a statement is false, it returns a different value. The whole functionality helps you compare a value and your prediction.

The IF function accepts the following inputs.

=IF [Value if true], [Value if false] in a logical text

- Logical text is the value or logical expression that must be evaluated and classified as TRUE or FALSE (Required Argument).
- Value if accurate (Probable Defense). When the outcome of the reasonable evaluation is TRUE, this value will be shown.
- Value if false (Possible Argument) will be returned if the rational assessment yields a FALSE result.

These logical operators can be used for this function:

Equal to (=)
Greater than (>)
Greater than or equal to (≥)
Less than (<)
Less than or equal to (≤)
Not equal (≠)

Verify that the value in cell A2 is more than 500. **=IF (Yes"**
and "No"; A2>500)

	A	B	C	D	E	F	G	H	I
SUM			fx	=IF(A2>500, "Yes", "No")					
1	Price	Result							
2	400	=IF(A2>500, "Yes", "No")							
3	800								
4	212								
5	454								
6	789								
7									
8									
9									
10									

Follow the instructions above to get the value of A3 to B6:
A3>500, "Yes", "No," A4>500, "Yes," "No," A5>500, and
A6>500, "Yes," "No," respectively.

	A	B	C	D	E	F	G	H	I
B6			fx	=IF(A6>500, "Yes", "No")					
1	Price	Result							
2	400	No							
3	800	Yes							
4	212	No							
5	454	No							
6	789	Yes							
7									
8									
9									
10									

8.2 IFERROR Function

When a formula fails, the IFERROR function creates a unique answer. The IFERROR records and manages errors instead of nested IF statements.

These are the parameters that the IFERROR utilizes.

(Value, value if error) =IFERROR

Value (Required Argument): It's a concept or utterance that has been examined or faults found.

Value if error (Required Argument): If there is a mistake in the formula, the value will be returned.

Let's use the IFERROR function to add a customized message that reads "invalid data" instead of the errors in the table below.

To fix the issue in cell C2, adhere to the methods listed below.

- Write the function's name and its arguments in a blank cell.

A2/B2, "invalid data," =IFERROR

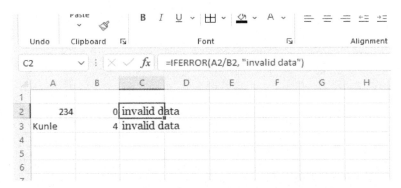

8.3 AND Function

The AND function examines if the conditions provided in a data set are TRUE, yielding a FALSE result if all conditions are not satisfied; for instance, B1 is more than 50 and less than 100.

The AND function is called with the following inputs.

(logical1, [logical2],) = AND

Logical1 (Necessary Argument): The first standard or logical value to be determined.

Logical2 (Optional Argument): A logical value is the second state of being evaluated.

To get the table's results, as previously described.

- Write the function's name and its arguments in a blank cell.

A2 > 67, A2 > A3

=AND(A2>67,A2<A3)

◢	A	B	C	D
1				
2	23	FALSE		
3	56			
4				

The AND function in the table above returns FALSE because one of the conditions in the data set, i.e., A2 is not greater than 67, was not satisfied.

As can be seen in the table below, the AND feature returns TRUE when the dataset requirements are satisfied.

	=AND(A2>20,A2<A3)			
	A	B	C	D
1				
2	23	TRUE		
3	56			
4				

8.4 OR Function

If all requirements are met, the OR function returns TRUE; otherwise, it returns FALSE. The result is returned as FALSE if any prerequisites are not met, in contrast to the AND function.

The following are the parameters for the OR function:

Logic 1 and Logic 2 (Required Argument): The first requirement or logical value to be established is = OR logical1.

Logical (Necessary argument): The second necessity is to establish the validity of the reasoning.

To get the outcomes shown in the table above.

Type **=OR(A2>30, B2>50, B3=45)**, enter the function's name and input parameters in a blank area.

The answer will be FALSE when you hit **Enter**, as seen below.

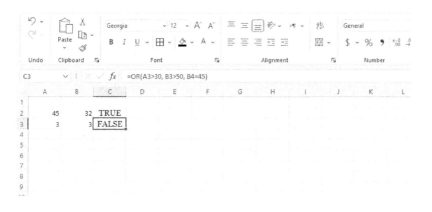

Chapter 9: Excel Statistical Functions

A spreadsheet function known as a statistical function performs mathematical calculations or other procedures on a set of cells. Future versions of Excel will have statistical capabilities. Examples are the statistical functions COUNT, COUNTA, AVERAGE, and others.

9.1 COUNT Function

The COUNT function refers to the overall number of arguments with numbers and the number of cells with numbers.

The COUNT function accepts the following parameters:

Value 1 (Required Support): The cell range for which you want to count the numbers is shown above.

Value2 (Exclusive Argument): can now include 255 more objects, numerical values, or spans for digit counting.

Applying COUNT

Let's count the number of cells in the table that contain numbers using the COUNT function.

	A	B	C	D	E
1	Goods Purchased	Price			
2	Jugs	450			
3	Pots	500			
4	Cuttleries	600			
5	Spoon	?			
6					
7					

- Choose a blank cell, then enter the function name and arguments. COUNT= (A2:B5)
- If you press **Enter**, you will get the number 3.

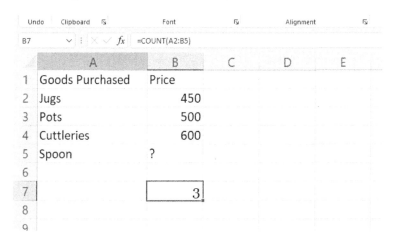

Use the COUNT tool while keeping these things in mind.

- The COUNT feature counts arguments that include numbers, dates, or language that denotes numbers.
- The COUNT function does not count typographical mistakes or value arguments.
- Make use of the COUNTA function to count logical values.
- The COUNTAIF or IF functions may count numbers depending on parameters.
- The COUNT function does not count TRUE and FALSE as rational values.
- When a statement is an index or array, just the numbers in the database or reference are added up.

9.2 COUNTIF Function

How many cells satisfy a given set of criteria is determined using the COUNTIF function. Dates, numerals, and text-containing cells may all be counted using this method. You may also use wildcards and logical operators with this feature.

The following parameters are accepted by the COUNTIF method:

=COUNTIF (Range, criteria)

Range (Required Argument): This specifies the cell range shown.

Criteria (Compulsory Argument): This is the prerequisite that each worksheet cell must meet. Here are a few examples of criteria:

Examples of numerical values are integer, decimal, temporal, and logical.

- East, Monday A text string containing wildcards like asterisks or question marks is an example of price.

Application of COUNTIF

Let's count how many times James' name appears in the column below using the COUNTIF function.

Follow the instructions below to find out how many times James' name appears on the page.

- Type the function's name and the required arguments in an empty box. James **=COUNTIF (B2:B6; James); =COUNTIF (B2:B6; James); =COUNTIF (B2;**

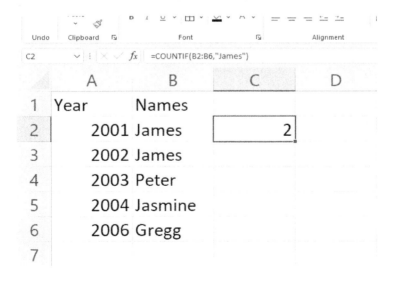

When using the COUNTIF tool, bear the following in mind.

- Please check that the criterion statement is included in quotes, such as "James," using the COUNTIF function.
- A #VALUE ERROR occurs when the given criterion statement is a text string longer than 255 characters.
- When a formula refers to a cell or a range of cells in a closed workbook, a #VALUE error occurs in that group of cells.

9.3 Average Function

A worksheet will utilize the AVERAGE equation to get the arithmetic mean of several inputs. 255 arguments may be sent to the AVERAGE function, including cell references, ranges, arrays, and constants.

The following parameters are used to invoke the **AVERAGE** function:

Number1 (Mandatory Argument): The first number in a cell relation or set that should be used to calculate the average.

Number2 (Supplementary Argument): Any extra numbers, cell comparisons, or ranges up to 255 characters long for which the average should be calculated.

Application of Average

Using the AVERAGE equation, calculate the arithmetic mean of the items sold in the table below.

	A	B	C	D
1	COUNTRIES	GOODS SOLD		
2	GHANA	400		
3	NIGERIA	600		
4	KENYA	698		
5	GAMBIA	543		
6				

Use the AVERAGE function following the steps below to get the average number of items sold.

Type the function name and arguments into a blank cell.

=AVERAGE (B2:B5)

When using the AVERAGE function, keep this in mind.

- The AVERAGE function does not consider empty cells.
- The AVERAGE function disregards text or logical values in a cell reference statement. On the other hand, cells with a value of 0 are counted.
- Numbers must be used in the parameters for the cell relation.
- Utilizing the AVERAGE function to estimate the number of logical values and textual representations of numbers.
- Use the AVERAGE IF or AVERAGE IFS functions to determine the average of any characteristic that fulfills a set of conditions or parameters.

Chapter 10: Excel Text Functions & Lookup Reference

Use the lookup functions for information from a list of data or tables on worksheets or workbooks. VLOOKUP, VLOOKUP, and other lookup functions are examples.

The Reference functions display text values that include information about a cell's reference, such as the whole address, row, and column. ADDRESS, ROW, and other functions serve as placeholders for these functions.

Let's quickly review the search and comparison tools and their potential spreadsheet applications.

10.1 VLOOKUP Function

It is simple to look up a piece of data in the first column of a table or dataset using the VLOOKUP function, which stands for "vertical lookup," and to obtain or return comparable information and data from a different column of the data set or table in the same row.

The VLOOKUP function operates with the parameters:

=VLOOKUP (col index num, [range lookup], table array, lookup value)

Look-up value (Required argument): The value to look up in the table's or dataset's first column.

Table array (Required Parameter): The data array that the lookup value in the column's leftmost section may search through.

Col index num (Needed Parameter): The table shows column numbers or integers where similar statistics are provided.

Range lookup (Optional parameter): Whether VLOOK can discover an exact or a good match depends on this code. Either TRUE or FALSE determines the statement's value. The next highest value is returned if a suitable match cannot be found. FALSE indicates an exact match, and #N/A is returned as an error if none is discovered.

The steps listed below may be used to utilize this function to get the value of yam in the table above:

- Choose an empty cell, then type the lookup value method, that is, the cell containing the desired data. The lookup cell in this instance is A12, which has the formula Yam =VLOOKUP (A12)

10.2 HLOOKUP Function

The HLOOKUP function, which stands for "horizontal lookup," is a device for retrieving a value or a piece of information from the top row of a table array or dataset and returning it together with another row's given value or item in the same column.

The HLOOKUP function uses the following inputs to conduct its job.

(Lookup value, table array, row index number, [range lookup]) = HLOOKUP

Follow the instructions below to calculate your overall Joy in Mathematics score.

Select a blank cell, then enter the lookup value or the cell containing the data to be searched for.

The lookup cell in this instance is B1, which contains the name. Pleasure; =HLOOKUP (B1

	A	B	C	D	E	F	G	H	I
1	Student Scores	Joy	Loveth	Jhon	Adex				
2	Maths		59	45	68	98			
3	English		69	78	43	76			
4	Economics		34	56	65	89			
5	Phe		23	89	24	97			
6									
7									
8	The Tptap Score of Joy in Mathematics	=HLOOKUP(B1							
9		HLOOKUP(lookup_value, table_array, row_index_num, [range_lookup])							
10									
11									

Finally, selecting **TRUE** or **FALSE** may inform Excel whether you're looking for an exact or perfect match.

=HLOOKUP or =HLOOKUP (B1, A1:E5, 3, FALSE) (B1, A1:E5,3, TRUE)

SUM =HLOOKUP(B1, A1:E5,2, FALSE)

	A	B	C	D	E	F	G	H	I
1	Student Scores	Joy	Loveth	Jhon	Adex				
2	Maths	59	45	68	98				
3	English	69	78	43	76				
4	Economics	34	56	65	89				
5	Phe	23	89	24	97				
6									
7									
8	The Tptap Score of Joy in Mathematics	=HLOOKUP(B1, A1:E5,2, FALSE)							
9		HLOOKUP(lookup_value, table_array, row_index_num, [range_lookup])							
10									
11									
12									

10.3 TRANSPOSE Function

The TRANSPOSE function is a technique for changing the orientation of a spectrum or array. A horizontal range may be transformed into a vertical range, and vice versa.

There is just one parameter needed for the TRANSPOSE operation. =TRANSPOSE (array)

Selecting any empty cells is the first step. Make sure the numbers in the chosen cells are arranged in the same sequence as the numbers in the cell's initial set.

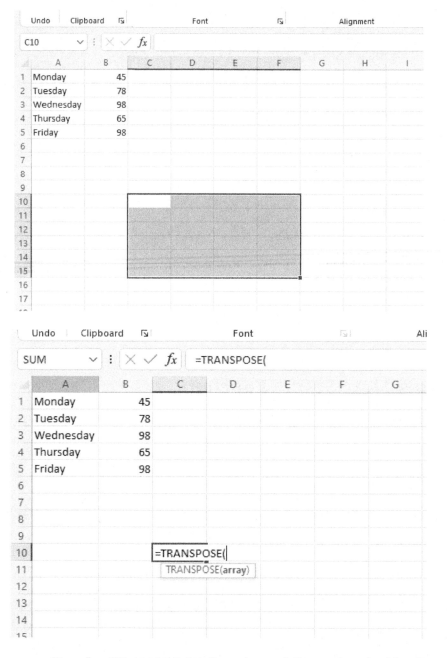

- Use the TRANSPOSE function while typing inside the context of the first set of cells.

| SUM | ⌄ | : | ✕ ✓ | fx | =TRANSPOSE(A1:B5) |

	A	B	C	D	E	F	G	H
1	Monday	45						
2	Tuesday	78						
3	Wednesday	98						
4	Thursday	65						
5	Friday	98						
6								
7								
8								
9								
10			=TRANSPOSE(A1:B5)					
11								
12								

- Finally, to transpose the chosen cell range, use CTRL+SHIF+ENTER.

| C11 | ⌄ | : | ✕ ✓ | fx | =TRANSPOSE(A1:B5) |

	A	B	C	D	E	F	G	H
1	Monday	45						
2	Tuesday	78						
3	Wednesday	98						
4	Thursday	65						
5	Friday	98						
6								
7								
8								
9								
10			Monday	Tuesday	Wednesd;	Thursday	Friday	
11			45	78	98	65	98	
12								
13								
14								

10.4 TRIM Function

The TRIM function removes extra spaces from a letter, leaving just one space between each word and no place for characters at the beginning or end. The TRIM function uses the following statements to perform its functions.

To eliminate the white space from the table's text.

- Write the goal and the defense in a blank cell. **=TEXTJOIN (",", TRUE, A2, A3, A4, A5, A6)**.

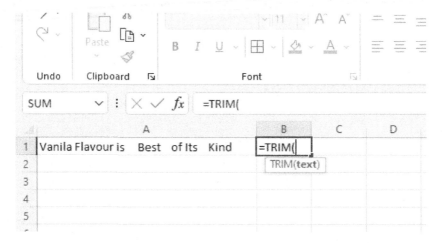

- The texts will be combined into a single string when you press enter, as seen below.

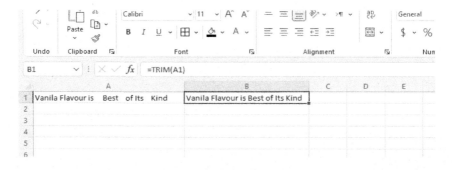

10.5 TEXTJOIN Function

Data from different cells or ranges are combined using the TEXTJOIN function by splitting each value with a delimiter. This is a brand-new feature in Microsoft Excel 2022. The procedures of the TEXTJOIN function are as follows.

Delimiter, ignore empty, text1, [text2], =TEXTJOIN, ...

Connect the texts in the table using the TEXTJOIN FUNCTION.

Select an empty cell type and its parameter **=TEXTJOIN** in the function (**",", TRUE, A2, A3, A4, A5, A6**)

When you click **Enter**, the texts will be concatenated into a single text string.

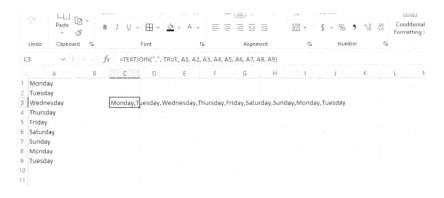

10.6 PROPER Function

The PROPER function reverses the cast of characters or text. The words preceding the capital letter in each text series are lowercase.

Only one parameter is required for the PROPER function. To modify the case of text strings, use =PROPER(Text)

- In a blank box, type the purpose and the defense.
  =PROPER(A2)

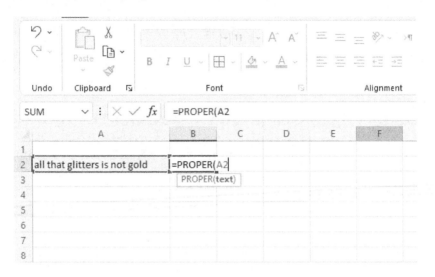

The text strings are changed to the appropriate case when you press enter, as shown below.

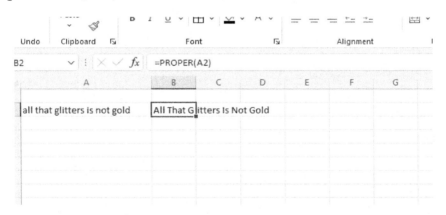

10.7 LOWER Function

A text string or cell reference may be converted to lowercase text characters using the LOWER capability.

This method only accepts one parameter, which is =LOWER(Text). Use the LOWER function to convert the characters in the table to lowercase.

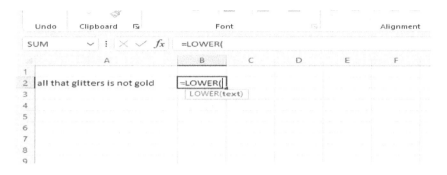

Use the LOWER feature to modify text strings as follows:

- Put the goal and the defense in an empty cell marked =LOWER (A2).

When you press enter, the text strings in the table below will be changed to lowercase.

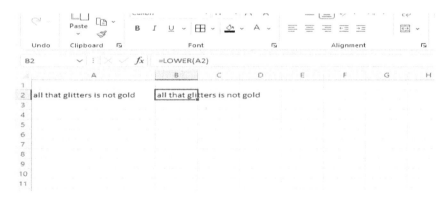

Chapter 11: Some Additional Features of Excel

You will learn about some shortcut keys to work faster when using excel to save your time and an exciting power view feature of Excel.

11.1 Excel Power View

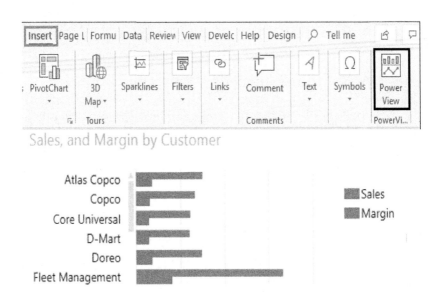

Sales, and Margin by Customer

You may create visually appealing charts and graphs, management dashboards, and reports that can be sent daily, weekly, or monthly using Excel's Power View function. This program may be a reporting tool in Excel and is compatible with Office 365 and all recent versions of Excel.

When you think about Excel, you see a variety of tools, such as PowerPivot, which enables users to draw knowledge from several databases and merge it into a single data set, and Formulae, PivotTables, and Analytical Tool-Pack, which simplify things for the analyst. In this chapter, you'll learn about a tool called Power View.

How to Enable Power View under Microsoft Excel?

You must first turn on Excel's Power View feature to create interactive reports and dashboards. Take the next actions:

- First, choose **Options** from the **File** menu by clicking on it.

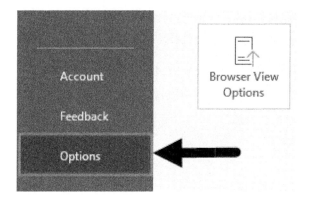

The **Excel Options** box has several options. Click on the **Add-ins** icon to see all add-in options.

The **Manage** option under **Add-ins** presents all Excel add-ins as a drop-down menu in this area. Select **Manage: COM Add-ins**, and then click the **Go** button.

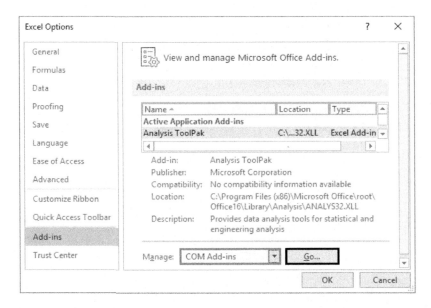

Finally, choose **Microsoft Power View for Excel** from the
COM Add-ins tab by clicking the **OK** button.

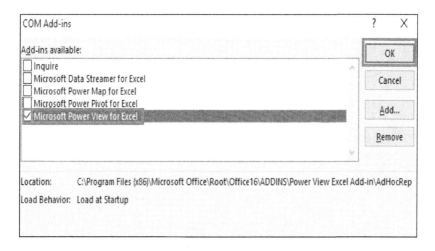

Consequently, Excel's **Power View** option will be enabled.
Access to the same is available through the **Insert** tab.

Example – Power View Usage in Excel

You have sales information you wish to examine from several
customers in different countries. You should use this data to
build a dashboard using **Power View**. The guidelines are as
follows:

	A	B	C	D	E	F
1	Date	Country	Customer	Quantity	Sales	Margin
2	1/1/2018	Dubai	Rehanmettal	1000	22000	7480
3	1/1/2018	India	Copco	1500	123200	43120
4	1/1/2018	India	Fleet Management	1500	44800	11200
5	1/2/2018	Oman	yale	2000	93500	31790
6	1/2/2018	Dubai	Atlas Copco	700	48800	6832
7	1/2/2018	Saudi Arabia	Doreo	500	9200	1288
8	1/3/2018	Saudi Arabia	LANDOLL	599	15000	2100
9	1/3/2018	Saudi Arabia	LANDOLL	140	9500	1710
10	1/5/2018	India	Copco	1500	56000	14560
11	1/5/2018	Saudi Arabia	D-Mart	1200	32500	9425
12	1/5/2018	Dubai	Core Universal	1350	106400	20216
13	1/5/2018	Saudi Arabia	Doreo	800	12600	3780
14	1/6/2018	Oman	yale	1120	14400	3312
15	1/6/2018	Saudi Arabia	D-Mart	1570	58500	21645

Before doing anything more, an Excel table must be created for all this data. By using **CTRL+T** and **OK**, you may insert a table.

	A	B	C	D	E	F
1	Date	Country	Customer	Quantity	Sales	Margin
2	1/1/2018	Dubai	Rehanmettal	1000	22000	7480
3	1/1/2018	India	Copco	1500	123200	43120
4	1/1/2018	India	Fleet Management	1500	44800	11200
5	1/2/2018			2000	93500	31790
6	1/2/2018			700	48800	6832
7	1/2/2018	S		500	9200	1288
8	1/3/2018	S		599	15000	2100
9	1/3/2018	S		140	9500	1710
10	1/5/2018			1500	56000	14560
11	1/5/2018			1200	32500	9425
12	1/5/2018	Dubai	Core Universal	1350	106400	20216
13	1/5/2018	Saudi Arabia	Doreo	800	12600	3780
14	1/6/2018	Oman	yale	1120	14400	3312
15	1/6/2018	Saudi Arabia	D-Mart	1570	58500	21645

Create Table dialog:
Where is the data for your table?
=$A$1:$F$1001
☑ My table has headers
OK   Cancel

The table should look as seen in the picture below:

	A	B	C	D	E	F
1	Date	Country	Customer	Quantity	Sales	Margin
2	1/1/2018	Dubai	Rehanmettal	1000	22000	7480
3	1/1/2018	India	Copco	1500	123200	43120
4	1/1/2018	India	Fleet Management	1500	44800	11200
5	1/2/2018	Oman	yale	2000	93500	31790
6	1/2/2018	Dubai	Atlas Copco	700	48800	6832
7	1/2/2018	Saudi Arabia	Doreo	500	9200	1288
8	1/3/2018	Saudi Arabia	LANDOLL	599	15000	2100
9	1/3/2018	Saudi Arabia	LANDOLL	140	9500	1710
10	1/5/2018	India	Copco	1500	56000	14560
11	1/5/2018	Saudi Arabia	D-Mart	1200	32500	9425
12	1/5/2018	Dubai	Core Universal	1350	106400	20216
13	1/5/2018	Saudi Arabia	Doreo	800	12600	3780
14	1/6/2018	Oman	yale	1120	14400	3312
15	1/6/2018	Saudi Arabia	D-Mart	1570	58500	21645

Next, choose **Power View** options from the list at the end of the **Insert** tab on Excel's ribbon.

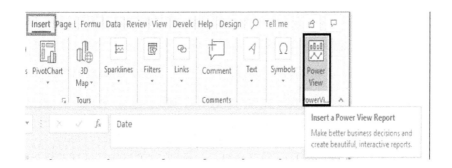

The **Power View Report** should be created in the same worksheet as soon as you make your Power View selection. The Power View arrangement may take some time to load, so we ask for your patience. The Power View summary will look something like this:

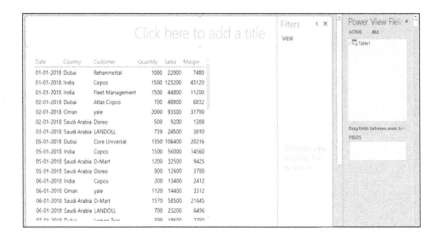

This report type features a table within the main report template, filters to the side, and a **Power View Feature** list like that seen in **PivotTables** in the top right corner. The report data may be further broken-down using filters and a Power View Feature list.

The fourth and last phase is selecting **Table 1** in **Power View Fields**, then selecting the **Country & Margin** columns from each drop-down box. The symbol for the **Sales**, **Quantity**, and **Margin** columns could be visible. It's there because those columns have numeric data that may be summed.

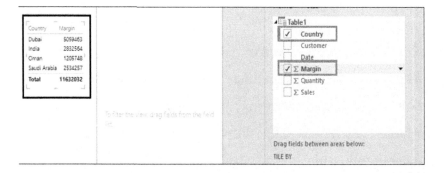

A new layout would be created using a **Power View Report** identical to that one.

The sixth step is this. We'll now include a graph for this country-by-country data in the data collection. Under the **Design** tab at the top of your ribbon, **Power View Reports** provide various design options. One of them is **Switch Visualization**. This option enables the **Power View Reports** to include graphs.

By choosing **Pie** from the **Other Chart** drop-down box, you may input a pie chart with data unique to a certain nation.

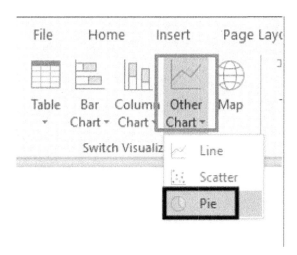

An example of how your chart may appear is as follows:

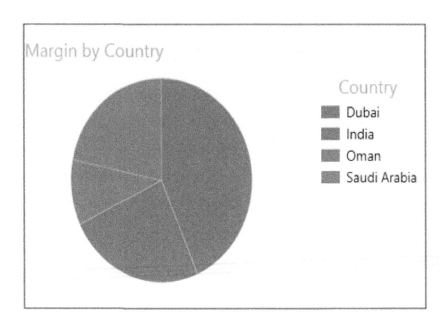

Select next the **Customer**, **Sales**, and **Margin** columns as your analysis inputs.

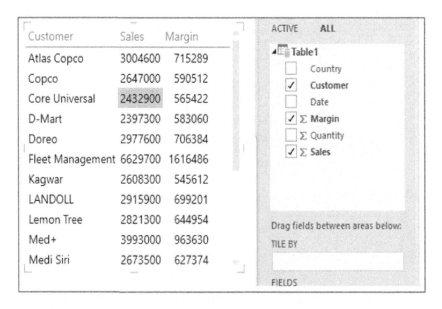

Go to the **Design** tab in **Switch Visualization** and choose a **Clustered** bar from the **Bar Chart** list.

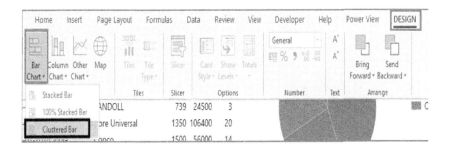

With this choice, you can see your customers' sales and profit margins in a single location. Here is a screenshot for your review:

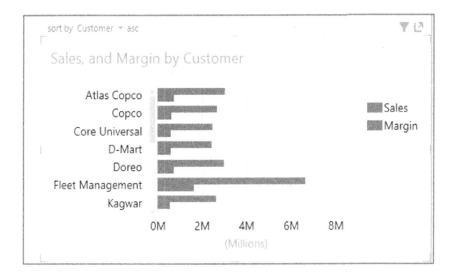

To reach the bottom of the list, use the scroll bar. Customer, sales, or margin may also sort the chart data. This graph reveals which customers provide us with the most revenue and profit margins.

This is the last action. The chart option will be used this time for both **Customer** & **Quantity**. Click on the two columns you wish to display in **Power View Fields**.

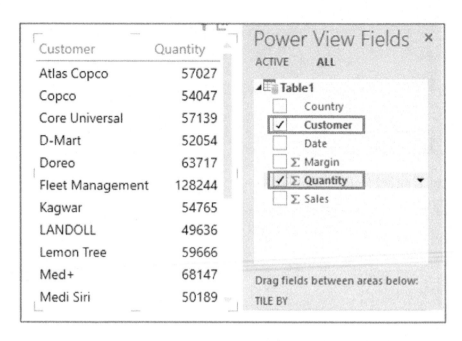

View the customer-wise bar chart sales by following the instructions in step 8. The graph should ideally look like this:

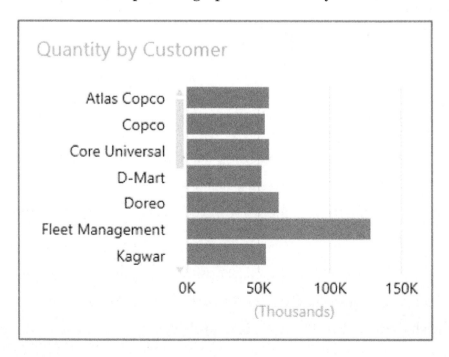

This graph reveals which customers purchased the most goods from you.

You may now deem this report to be finished. Please title this report **"Sales Comparison with Different Parameters.**"

The following screenshot displays the final layout of your Power View Report:

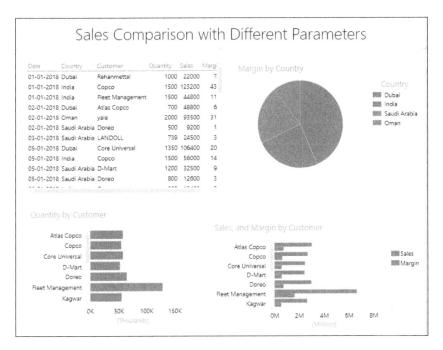

11.2 Excel Shortcuts

Need for Excel Shortcuts

Excel keyboard shortcuts let you work more quickly and efficiently. The toolbar may be accessed with 2 or 3 keystrokes rather than a mouse, which saves time. Don't you save a ton of time and work by doing that? Excel shortcuts accelerate the procedure, reducing the time needed to finish a job.

The answer to whether mastering these shortcuts is required is no. However, you'll have an advantage if you remember a few. After a lot of practice, you'll be able to remember the majority of the fundamental Excel shortcuts.

Let's review the top 50 Excel shortcuts that every user should know. 50 Excel shortcuts have been divided into groups based on their intended application. We'll start by looking at the worksheet's shortcut keys.

Workbook Shortcut Keys

Using a workbook is simple once you understand the basics. You'll discover how to create a new workbook, load any other workbook, and save a spreadsheet. After that, you'll look at utilizing the tab key to navigate between different worksheet pages.

Description	Excel Shortcuts
1. To create a new workbook	Ctrl + N
2. To open an existing workbook	Ctrl + O
3. To save a workbook/spreadsheet	Ctrl + S
4. To close the current workbook	Ctrl + W
5. To close Excel	Ctrl + F4
6. To move to the next sheet	Ctrl + PageDown
7. To move to the previous sheet	Ctrl + PageUp
8. To go to the Data tab	Alt + A
9. To go to the View tab	Alt + W
10. To go the Formula tab	Alt + M

Now that you've discovered some helpful Excel shortcuts, put your spreadsheet out of your mind. The next step after creating a workbook is to format the cells.

Cell Formatting Shortcut Keys

All the data you're dealing with right now in Excel is contained in a cell. When editing cells, you may use several conveniences, such as aligning the contents of the cells and adding borders. Applying a border to all chosen cells is another option. The following list of Excel keyboard shortcuts is provided.

Description	Excel Shortcuts
11. To edit a cell	F2
12. To copy and paste cells	Ctrl + C, Ctrl + V
13. To italicize and make the font bold	Ctrl + I, Ctrl + B
14. To center align cell contents	Alt + H + A + C
15. To fill color	Alt + H + H
16. To add a border	Alt + H + B
17. To remove outline border	Ctrl + Shift + _
18. To add an outline to the select cells	Ctrl + Shift + &
19. To move to the next cell	Tab
20. To move to the previous cell	Shift + Tab
21. To select all the cells on the right	Ctrl + Shift + Right arrow
22. To select all the cells on the left	Ctrl + Shift + Left Arrow
23. To select the column from the selected cell to the end of the table	Ctrl + Shift + Down Arrow
24. To select all the cells above the selected cell	Ctrl + Shift + Up Arrow
25. To select all the cells below the selected cell	Ctrl + Shift + Down Arrow

Let's look at a few more advanced Excel shortcuts for formatting cells and the ones we've previously covered.

In this session, you will discover how to create a cell remark. Comments may help describe a cell's content in greater detail. You would be able to identify a value and then swap it out for another using the spreadsheet.

Let's start with the basics: how to enter the current time and date, enable a filter, and add an interactive hyperlink to a single cell. The final format will be that of the data contained inside a cell.

Description	Excel Shortcuts
26. To add a comment to a cell	Shift + F2
27. To delete a cell comment	Shift + F10 + D
28. To display find and replace	Ctrl + H
29. To activate the filter	Ctrl + Shift + L Alt + Down Arrow
30. To insert the current date	Ctrl + ;
31. To insert current time	Ctrl + Shift + :
32. To insert a hyperlink	Ctrl + k
33. To apply the currency format	Ctrl + Shift + $
34. To apply the percent format	Ctrl + Shift + %
35. To go to the "Tell me what you want to do" box	Alt + Q

The next stage is to learn how to work with an entire row or column in Excel after dealing with the cell formatting shortcuts in the application.

Row and Column Formatting Shortcut Keys

Several significant shortcuts for formatting rows and columns will be taught to you.

In this chapter, you will learn how to hide and then re-show the selected columns and rows and delete whole rows and columns.

Description	Excel Shortcuts
36. To select the entire row	Shift + Space
37. To select the entire column	Ctrl + Space
38. To delete a column	Alt+H+D+C
39. To delete a row	Shift + Space, Ctrl + -
40. To hide selected row	Ctrl + 9
41. To unhide selected row	Ctrl + Shift + 9
42. To hide a selected column	Ctrl + 0
43. To unhide a selected column	Ctrl + Shift + 0
44. To group rows or columns	Alt + Shift + Right arrow
45. To ungroup rows or columns	Alt + Shift + Left arrow

After learning about the numerous shortcuts for formatting cells, rows, and columns in Microsoft Excel, you're prepared to move on to more complicated ideas, such as pivot tables. You may use the pivot table to summarize your data in several ways.

Pivot Table Shortcut Keys

Create a pivot table first using the sales data.

Under each product category, a pivot table summarizing overall sales with each product subcategory is available for viewing.

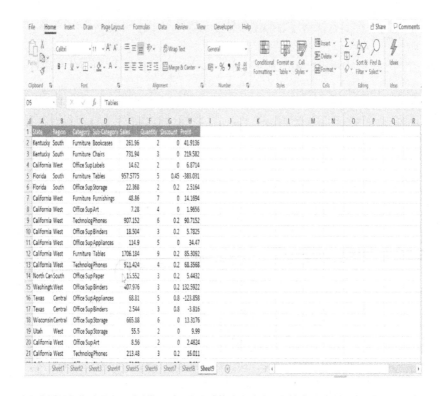

State	Region	Category	Sub-Category	Sales	Quantity	Discount	Profit
Kentucky	South	Furniture	Bookcases	261.96	2	0	41.9136
Kentucky	South	Furniture	Chairs	731.94	3	0	219.582
California	West	Office Sup	Labels	14.62	2	0	6.8714
Florida	South	Furniture	Tables	957.5775	5	0.45	-383.031
Florida	South	Office Sup	Storage	22.368	2	0.2	2.5164
California	West	Furniture	Furnishings	48.86	7	0	14.1694
California	West	Office Sup	Art	7.28	4	0	1.9656
California	West	Technolog	Phones	907.152	6	0.2	90.7152
California	West	Office Sup	Binders	18.504	3	0.2	5.7825
California	West	Office Sup	Appliances	114.9	5	0	34.47
California	West	Furniture	Tables	1706.184	9	0.2	85.3092
California	West	Technolog	Phones	911.424	4	0.2	68.3568
North Can	South	Office Sup	Paper	15.552	3	0.2	5.4432
Washingt	West	Office Sup	Binders	407.976	3	0.2	132.5922
Texas	Central	Office Sup	Appliances	68.81	5	0.8	-123.858
Texas	Central	Office Sup	Binders	2.544	3	0.8	-3.816
Wisconsin	Central	Office Sup	Storage	665.88	6	0	13.3176
Utah	West	Office Sup	Storage	55.5	2	0	9.99
California	West	Office Sup	Art	8.56	2	0	2.4824
California	West	Technolog	Phones	213.48	3	0.2	16.011

46. To group pivot table items   **Alt + Shift + Right arrow**

The graph below shows that sales of chairs and bookcases fall within Group 1.

47. To ungroup pivot table items   **Alt + Shift + Left arrow**
48. To hide pivot table items   **Ctrl + -**

You'll see that you've hidden the subcategories for Chairs, Art, and Labels on this page.

Row Labels	Sum of Sales
Furniture	741999.7953
Bookcases	114879.9963
Chairs	328449.103
Furnishings	91705.164
Tables	206965.532
Office Supplies	719047.032
Appliances	107532.161
Art	27118.792
Binders	203412.733
Envelopes	16476.402
Fasteners	3024.28
Labels	12486.312
Paper	78479.206
Storage	223843.608
Supplies	46673.538
Technology	836154.033
Accessories	167380.318
Copiers	149528.03
Machines	189238.631

Row Labels	Sum of Sales
Furniture	413550.6923
Bookcases	114879.9963
Furnishings	91705.164
Tables	206965.532
Office Supplies	679441.928
Appliances	107532.161
Binders	203412.733
Envelopes	16476.402
Fasteners	3024.28
Paper	78479.206
Storage	223843.608
Supplies	46673.538
Technology	836154.033
Accessories	167380.318
Copiers	149528.03
Machines	189238.631
Phones	330007.054
Grand Total	1929146.653

49. To create a pivot chart on the same sheet	Alt + F1
50. To create a pivot chart on a new worksheet	F11

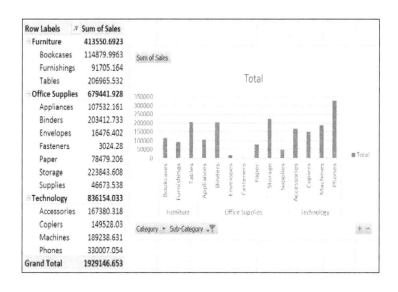

The creation of reports and analysis might be sped using Excel shortcut keys. After reading this guide, you should know several Excel shortcuts related to workbooks, cell formatting, row & column formatting, and pivot tables.

Chapter 12: What Are the Most Desired Excel Abilities for a Job?

You'll need education, whether you're seeking work or thinking about changing your profession.

You'll need to know how to use a computer and be comfortable with Microsoft Excel to do even the most elementary tasks. The job shouldn't be entirely out of the question if you're a beginner at Excel programming. Even if you've never used Excel professionally, you should at least have a basic understanding of the application when applying for a job that calls for it.

What are the most in-demand Excel abilities?

Below is a list of necessary professional credentials and some fundamental Excel expertise.

12.1 Knowledge of Advanced Excel Functions

Excel's main objective is to make it simple to automate tasks that would otherwise take a lot of human effort via the use of built-in functions. Excel functions may be used to solve compound hitches; you only need a few fundamental skills with the spreadsheet tool.

Employers would highly value your skills if you can utilize Excel's advanced functions to apply or design them for any notion. Because they feel that employees are worthless and useless without this knowledge, employers are unwilling to keep their workforce.

12.2 Placement of Various Functions

As you learn the ropes, the default output result for most Excel functions is one cell. But there is also another sector where complex features are in use. Rearranging the axes of your data is one of the most often utilized functions. To successfully organize these functions in Excel, one must have a thorough understanding of all the functions and strong Excel skills.

12.3 Separation of Data and Corresponding Entries

Excel users must have a solid understanding of the fundamentals of the program's operation, but this isn't the only ability you should seek to hone. Spreadsheet work demands closeness. A worker must be used to setting up and arranging the cells and figures of tablets daily.

This includes several sophisticated Excel features and abilities, such as sorting data and adding and removing connected things in Excel. Excel includes a variety of features that anybody may thoroughly research.

12.4 Making Use of Appropriate Data Validation Methods

The personnel must be aware of Excel sheet limits in several circumstances. The description of the development of cell drop-down lists is made possible by data validation.

Employers often look for employees with practical experience in data validation, which allows users to verify drop-away range files containing the acceptable inputs for preset cells. Effective verification is required since every employer wants their job completed in their way and style.

12.5 Data Breakdown Provided

Several tools are available for Excel experienced users working with numbers to make their lives simpler while crunching data. Employers are seeking someone who can quickly secure and recover access to encrypted numbers because of this. Employees could be required to know who is appropriate to work with.

12.6 Mastery of the Command Line

Employees need to be able to create reports utilizing data forecasts, complete with manipulating graphs and charts. A basic level of this talent was covered in an Excel course. Throughout the employment process, employers are looking for this. The tools you employ should be dependable and well-thought-out if you offer commercial information.

12.7 Completeness of Information Formatting

Employers are looking for candidates with a solid grasp of Excel's many capabilities, including correctly aligning data, formatting data, and using all of Excel's built-in functions.

If the data is not presented appropriately and briefly, the presentation is insufficient and, consequently, is not worth exhibiting to management or customers. Every employee must know the proper data formatting logic for each project.

12.8 Informative Data about Excel's Primitive Formulas and Calculations

The ability to add and subtract formulas in Excel files and a solid understanding of basic mathematical concepts and calculations are two of the most crucial qualities employers look for when employing new staff. This is particularly true in large-scale business settings where it is necessary to manage several standards and reports in spreadsheets to get to a conclusion.

12.9 Display Formatting Options That Do Their Job

Users of spreadsheets should be aware of this crucial fact as well. This category will feature Excel actions that are used often but are rotated to change how the cells look other than how the spreadsheet is printed.

Any version of Excel allows users to alter the cell color and size, fonts outside borders, and cell dimensions. Any company seeking to recruit new personnel must visualize the organizational structure in the form of specific sheets, tables, or cells.

12.10 Acquaintance with Related Roles

Employers often look for candidates who are proficient in other pertinent activities. Excel's features provide security and a preview of what more experienced users may do with the different Excel series.

Excel, on the other hand, has far more possibilities. Just a few examples include pivot tables, numerous financial mock-up tools, and data referencing across panes and workbooks. Additionally, you must know all the associated hidden tricks for Excel functions.

These are some of the qualities that businesses often check when hiring someone for a corporate position. All you must do to improve your Excel skills is put what you've learned in the classroom into practice. A prospective employer places the most value on your ability to accomplish all required tasks without difficulty.

Chapter 13: High Salary Jobs with Excel Skills

All organizations must continually adapt and innovate to be relevant in today's global economy. By implementing training programs that assist your staff in staying current with the latest technology and doing their jobs more efficiently, you can maintain your business on top in several ways.

Through ongoing development and training, businesses may also protect one of their most valuable assets: their employees.

You won't be able to stay up with your workers if you don't push them hard enough. Giving workers the continuing training they need to be as effective as possible may help businesses boost staff retention, lower employee turnover, and lower the risk of losing their best workers to competitors. An application called Excel for Business is often included in numerous educational training courses.

These are the top seven occupations you can get after studying advanced Excel:

13.1 MIS Executive

Database management is the main responsibility of an MIS Executive. After maintaining the company's data, he is now in charge of giving it to his group and management, who often use MS Excel.

Since data management is essential to every company's future success, MIS executives are in great demand. If you're skilled with MS Excel, you'll be able to get a job and start earning your best money.

These are some examples of what an MIS executive's work entails.

- The main duty of an MIS Executive is to create routine, weekly, and monthly MIS reports.
- He must be able to collaborate with company data and create different reports.
- He must work with very complicated data sets.
- When working with enormous volumes of data, Advance Excel is a lifesaver.
- Serve as the team leader for the organization's records.
- The report must incorporate input from every employee.
- He uses Advance Excel to prepare a perfect report that he submits to the company's higher management.

13.2 Project Coordinator or manager

A program manager's main duty is supervising a particular business project from beginning to end. As the project manager, he supervises, plans, implements, and closes off ventures.

Project managers are thus required to possess excellent Excel skills. They should be able to arrange all their data more effectively if they want to make the most of their MS Excel skills.

What are a project manager's responsibilities and duties?

- The planning and implementation of the project
- Make sure the group is moving in the right direction.
- increased collaboration by monitoring every area of the project
- Reduce the time devoted to problem-solving
- Manage the budget needs of the project.
- Encourage and assist your coworkers.
- Set deadlines and keep an eye on the status of the project.

13.3 Market Research Analysis

The major responsibility of analysts is to thoroughly examine diverse items. As a result, a researcher with expertise in market research gathers information to support businesses with their extensive marketing initiatives. Market analysts are essential if a company outperforms its competitors in the marketplace.

Customers, prices, and sales are all monitored by them. They establish trusting relationships with their clients so they may find out what they like and don't like. This procedure might be made a lot simpler by using MS Excel.

What is a market research analyst's responsibility?

- Research the market as thoroughly as you can.
- Utilize Microsoft Excel's organizational and analytical capabilities to arrange the data you've gathered.
- Graphs and charts may help you better understand data.

- Identify the company's position in the market.
- Find out what's fresh in the market.
- For the growth of your firm, analyze data.
- He researches the market and the competitors for the company's advantage.

13.4 Retail Store manager

An area where items are kept in inventory and utilized as required is a shop. Retailers purchase things in bulk and store them in a physical location. Retailers that purchase huge numbers directly from manufacturers sell smaller quantities to clients.

He receives an additional margin from the manufacturer when he purchases bulk. With advanced Excel knowledge, this task may be completed more quickly.

What are the responsibilities of retail store managers?

- He oversees the whole retail establishment.
- He examines a retail establishment's routine.
- He creates regulations that are advantageous to the retail industry.
- Assuming control over the store's personnel
- Making a complete inventory.
- Spending should be planned.
- Make a trend analysis.
- Increase your profit margin.

13.5 Business Analysts

A business analyst's main duty is to enhance the organization's procedures and IT infrastructure to boost sales. MS Excel proficiency is a must for business analysts to do their tasks efficiently and correctly.

Business analysts need to work with a lot of data to help the firm expand. Excel is the best tool for processing a lot of data because of its sophisticated capabilities.

What precisely do business analysts do for a living?

- Focus data analysis on the main objective of the business.
- creating innovative business strategies and controlling spending
- The most lucrative business segments for a corporation should be identified and used.
- implementing a plan determined by data analysis
- Be ready for novel methods.
- Create a record of the data analysis.
- Help the company make system improvements to enable future growth.

13.6 Data Journalists

By maintaining data on sales, client data, and marketing activities, a company may be built using its customers' profiles and marketing efforts. Additionally, the database includes division-by-division breakdowns of all the company's activities.

Each department should use it to its full potential to provide the best outcomes, avoid errors, and use fewer resources to fulfill deadlines. Data journalists need access to enormous volumes of data to suit the firm's needs.

What are the responsibilities and tasks of a Data Journalist?

- Large databases may be stored in Excel.
- Analyze the data to see what more you can discover.
- For data journalists, a spreadsheet in Excel might be an excellent place to start.
- Gather data to create reports.
- Improve your database knowledge
- Utilizing fiction to present information
- Create and edit content for various mediums.
- Make and manage databases utilizing Excel's more complex features.

13.7 Financial Analysts

By examining financial data, analysts help organizations make the best judgments possible. He'll need to be an expert user of Microsoft Excel to manipulate and save the data.

He has concluded from the financial data of the organization. Financial analysts provide suggestions to businesses on how to save expenses and increase profitability.

Do financial analysts do any tasks?

- Data analysis and financial research may both be done using MS Excel.
- Aid the company in making wise financial choices.
- Daily Excel updates are used
- He offers an Excel spreadsheet with the year's sales and profits.
- Watch your money in investing.
- Make an action plan based on the financial data.
- To provide reliable data, review and write a report.
- You may compile information using an MS Excel database.

Conclusion

In Excel, greater knowledge equates to more money. The same ideas apply to Excel as well. If you have a thorough understanding of Excel, you may get high-paying work in analytics. As you can see, Excel has a variety of uses. However, this manual's highlights were a few of them. There are many additional uses for the term "excellence."

Excel makes professional work easier. Even if you don't have a strong foundation in arithmetic or statistics, you can now complete a whole calculation. Only Microsoft Excel makes this even possible. Nobody wants to be the only one in the room unfamiliar with Microsoft Excel. With the assistance of our experts, you may get started with your Excel instruction right now.

Students and professionals may find it useful to learn the principles of MS Excel, a simple program, throughout their careers in various industries. Beginners, who may not be familiar with the software's more complex features, are likely to place the most significance on the most basic features, such as rows, columns, and tables. You must first have a thorough grasp of the platform and its advantages before using the app in the day-to-day operations of your firm.

Excel makes data entry straightforward is the biggest advantage of utilizing it. The MS Excel Ribbon design consists of instructions that may be used to complete basic activities and may replace many data entry and analysis procedures.

The tabs dispersed over the ribbon are where the command groups and corresponding keys are grouped. The arrangement of these tabs is tabbed. Selecting the appropriate tab may conduct tasks more quickly and pick instructions.

In general, Microsoft Excel helps you manipulate, monitor, and evaluate results, empowering you to make better choices and sparing you with money and time. Whether managing your finances or working on a project for your organization, Microsoft Excel provides the tools you need to get any job done.

Utilizing pre-existing templates to create customized spreadsheets for business needs, data interpretation, and multimedia statistical analysis is possible with this application.

Excel is a flexible program that may be used for analysis and what-if tests. Formulas within cells that accept one or more input cells must be used to calculate the various situations. Dealing with different values and choices may be simpler using the tools included in the Control toolbox or Forms toolbar. These settings will make it easier to utilize your models when used properly.

Frame the QR code with your smartphone

type your e-mail address and receive the BONUS:

https://tinyurl.com/bonusexcel

Printed in Great Britain
by Amazon